LOST
EDINBURGH

✳

LOST
EDINBURGH

✱

Hamish Coghill

BIRLINN

✳

This edition first published in 2008 by
Birlinn Limited
West Newington House
10 Newington Road
Edinburgh
EH9 1QS

www.birlinn.co.uk

Reprinted 2010, 2012, 2014, 2016

ISBN13: 978 1 84158 747 9

British Library Cataloguing-in-Publication Data
A catalogue record for this book is available
from the British Library

Designed and typeset by Mark Blackadder

Printed and bound by Gutenberg Press Ltd, Malta

*

*For Murray, Gregor, Isobel, Abegail and Alasdair,
and their Grandma, Mary*

CONTENTS

INTRODUCTION

Reverence for mere antiquity, and even for modern beauty,
on their own account, is scarcely a Scottish passion.

Lord Cockburn, *Memorials of His Time*, 1856

One cannot, however, expect to preserve everything if improvements
are to be made to meet present and future needs.

A Civic Survey and Plan for Edinburgh, 1949

The tourists who flock into Edinburgh in their hundreds of thousands every year gladly walk the Royal Mile between the Castle and the Palace of Holyroodhouse. They look at old buildings, peer into closes – those dark, narrow thoroughfares dividing the high structures – to see in some of them simply stumps of houses. They sense in the High Street and in the Canongate reconstruction a feeling of antiquity.

But how would they and Edinburghers feel if they could still explore the Old Tolbooth outside St Giles' Cathedral, or walk down the Parliament Stairs, loiter outside the French Ambassador's Chapel in the Cowgate or even take a bracing stroll along Portobello's Victorian pier?

In growing from a huddle of huts round a fortress on a volcanic rock into an international and cosmopolitan city, Edinburgh has had to change. And inevitably there will be more changes, if for nothing more than to meet the demand for more houses, more office space, bigger and better shopping centres, new roads and sports facilities. That is part of inhabitants' relentness demand on their city.

With the Old Town and New Town areas now a World Heritage Site, the worst destructive excesses of the past should not be allowed to occur again.

But what destruction Edinburgh has seen over the years, sometimes by enemy hand, often self-inflicted. Campaigns to conserve have been fought, occasionally won, more often lost, and another slice of the townscape has gone.

It is impossible to record every building which has been replaced over the centuries because in a changing city things can happen very quickly, not least when, as occurred on several occasions, it was put to the fire by English armies. Later, the Victorian 'improvers' and successive developers shared one thing – a burning desire to carry out their plans come what may. Anything that was in the way of a new street or bridge or civic development was knocked down.

When we talk of the New Town, we have to remember that the first houses were started there in 1767 – an initiative driven by men of vision who saw that the city had to be shaken out of its moribund stupor as buildings were literally tumbling down around the citizens' heads. But was it necessary a century later to be ripping away much of the medieval town?

Many of the once outlying village communities were also swallowed up by the expanding Edinburgh – or simply flattened. Where are the villages of Picardie or Broughton or St Ninian's Row now, for instance?

The 20th century saw a growing appreciation that buildings with a place in the city's history, for archaeological reasons or otherwise, deserved to be protected where possible, but George Square, for example, is a small shadow of itself and its 18th-century charm is lost to the present and future generations.

Changing demands have seen once-great industries, such as brewing and printing, shrink to an incredible degree in what was both a great brewing and printing centre, renowned throughout the world. Who now recalls Thomas Nelson's Parkside works, across the road from where the Royal Commonwealth Pool stands, and all the other famous printing houses? Who has swallowed all the ale-makers?

So many industrial or factory sites are now filled with flats. Even Powderhall Stadium, a multi-purpose sports ground, has fallen to the changing times and houses stand on the former greyhound track.

No longer do the mills on the Water of Leith clank in their sheltered vale. Again, the old buildings make good houses or, even better for the housebuilders, the cleared sites provide room for many homes. We have seen in recent years supermarkets built on sports fields, more houses on every spare corner, a resurgence in Leith Docks of super-development and the start of the process to transform the city's northern boundary in the Waterfront scheme. A successful fight was waged to save the local polo field at Colinton, Meadowbank Stadium looks like it has come to the end of its useful days, the characters like the one-man band or the hurdy-gurdy woman who once wandered the streets are no longer with us. Our old trams are mere memories, and the new tramway system, one of the most contentious issues in Edinburgh in recent years – truncated, over budget and years behind schedule – will never replace in our hearts the shoogly monsters of yesteryear.

In 2002, the frequent curse of Edinburgh – the raging inferno – ripped through a chunk of the Cowgate, necessitating the removal of the gutted remains in that street and up above on South Bridge. Another slice lost, but a challenge to planners and architects to combine a historical site with a worthy 21st-century renaissance.

This book aims to leave the reader with at least a flavour of what has been lost on the building front and concentrates on that aspect. Along the way, however, I hope it also gives something of the life of this old town.

There was immense building activity in the city during the early years of the 21st century, but the recession has certainly slowed potential development. The skyline, however, is punctured by cranes on various sites.

Significant archaeological finds have also been made in a re-examination of the Tron Kirk, where the original line of the High Street has been discovered, while the Cowgate fire-site discoveries have added significantly to our knowledge of the Old Town area.

Edinburgh does not stand still – the construction of the much talked about tramway has been completed; the transformation of the Fountainbridge and former Royal Infirmary areas is well under way; and on the shorelines the changes are very apparent.

Familiar buildings are lost, but I believe there is now a much greater appreciation of our architectural heritage, with people prepared to fight against unwanted and unwarranted developments. Long may that attitude continue.

Hamish Coghill
2014

Timber-fronted houses over arcaded galleries were the style of 16th- and 17th-century homes in Edinburgh. The houses were frequently the place of business with a workshop or brewhouse on the premises. The wooden arcades were later replaced by stone, a feature which can be seen in the original Gladstone's Land in the Lawnmarket and in the reconstruction of parts of the Canongate.

CHAPTER 1
PARADISE LOST

It was around 8500 BC that the earliest hunter-gatherers found a refuge on the banks of the River Almond, close to where the Romans were to form a settlement many hundreds of centuries later.

As they crouched over a fire, the women and children watching from rough shelters of branches and gorse, those pioneers could not have known that they were carving a way for what was to become the proud capital of a fiercely independent country. Those early travellers probably believed they had lost or left nothing as they moved on to the next campsite. But modern science has shown us that they did leave traces, now recognised more than 10,000 years later. From the shells of nuts they chewed, they left the earliest signs of man found to date in Scotland.

Their shelters are lost, but we are reminded that before Edinburgh became a small community, far less the capital of Scotland, home in two different epochs to a national Parliament and, since the late 1940s, to a world-renowned international festival of music and drama, people and things existed of which we are not yet aware. They come into the category of lost, but not yet found. That will be for future generations to discover, but already the 'lost' list in Edinburgh is a formidable one.

The causes are in the main: invasion, negligence, fire, pestilence, expansion and that most evocative but dangerous desire – 'improvement'.

For Edinburgh, 'improvements' have seen the sweeping away of many important buildings – some, like the Old Tolbooth in the High Street, rich in history, others, interesting houses in places like the Cowgate. The desire for progress, to push out the bounderies of a small medieval town clinging to the slopes of a ridge running from the Castle to the bottom of the Canongate meant, in a time when conservation and preservation carried little weight, that a vast amount was irretrievably lost. The early settlement of the Edinburgh area can be traced through the stone forts and houses of the Bronze and Iron Ages found

*Remains of a hill fort on Wester Craiglockhart Hill are a reminder
that the Edinburgh area has been inhabited for thousands of years.*

on the hills in Holyrood Park, Craiglockhart Hill and the Pentlands. There was a Roman occupation at Cramond at the mouth of the River Almond, and the bath-house which was built to let weary bones sweat the day's tiredness away and provide a welcome relief to bodies used to hardships and differing climes in the emperor's service is buried today beneath a car park.

But it is the Castle Rock which came to dominate – its importance as a place of relative safety being quickly recognised. The western summit of the crag and tail, created by a volcanic eruption millions of years ago, followed by the glaciers of the Ice Age, has always been a vital factor in the growth of the city, and as often as the fortress on it has been battered in invasion by the English or razed by the Scots themselves – Robert the Bruce ordered its demolition – it has risen phoenix-like to be the most recognisable and reassuring sight on the Edinburgh skyline.

Inevitably, much of Edinburgh's early development must be speculation, but from the seventh century there has been a fortress more or less continuously on the rock.

Its strategic importance was recognised earlier than that, however – in the Dark Ages:

> Among the numerous hill forts of that period in the region, Edinburgh alone commands the point where the Roman route from

the south reached the Firth of Forth [the Royal Commission on the Ancient Monuments of Scotland states in its inventory.] Here is then the appropriate point of concentration for trade and political influence, however irregular the one or shadowy the other, in an age when these things centred on a chieftain's stronghold.

The same factor guaranteed the site's future. The situation was bound to attract the Angles, whose realm of Bernica was ruled from a coastal fortress and owed its cohesion to a combined use of the North Sea and the arterial land route provided by Dere Street, the Roman road from the Tees to the Forth.

The Normans whose eye for a commanding position was even keener, must have been no less alive to the happy conjunction of advantages. Thus it is the relation of the site to the wreck of the Roman road system which is the key to Edinburgh's early importance, and the explanation of why Edinburgh lived when other Dark Age sites in Lothian, like Traprain and Kaims Hill, died out of existence.

The landscape those many centuries ago was markedly different – many stretches of fresh water lochs would be seen by the watchers on the big volcanic rock. They came to be known as the South Loch (drained to form the present-day Meadows), Corstorphine Loch, Gogar Loch, Craigcrook Loch, Canonmills Loch, Holyrood Loch, Blackford Loch and Jordanville Loch, among others. The stretch of Duddingston Loch which survives today was much larger, while the old Restalrig (now Lochend) Loch has also shrunk in area. Dunsapie Loch in Holyrood Park was affected by the improving zeal of Queen Victoria's Consort, Prince Albert, who had it enlarged. Originally, there was another water source in the area of Hunter's Bog in Holyrood Park, and in recent years a new loch has been formed there.

Virtually gone too is the once-sprawling Burgh Muir, which stretched from the banks of the South (or Burgh) Loch over the hill towards the modern Blackford Hill, and from Duddingston in the east to Tipperlinn in the west.

We will come later to another loch which was created as a defence – the Nor' Loch, which nestled beneath the Castle Rock in the valley which is now Princes Street Gardens and which also played a central role in the social life of the town.

As the Castle Rock became more of a fortress area, the houses were moved down the ridge of Castlehill, and it seems there was a definite pattern in the layout, with householders offered a 'toft', or stretch of garden and grazing ground, behind. The main street was 100 feet (30 metres) wide at the centre of the ridge. Former City Architect E. J. MacRae has described Edinburgh in 1329 as having no castle because Robert the Bruce had ordered its destruction, so that it would not again fall into the hands of the enemy English:

> Edinburgh was an unwalled burgh with its small houses on its High Street from Lawnmarket to Netherbow backed by their gardens interrupted by the ancient church of St Giles. A stream ran down each side of the ridge. Below the Castle Rock to the north-west was the church of St Cuthbert's, already in being at the time of the twelfth century charter to Holyrood Abbey. To the south and west of the Castle Rock were the King's gardens, orchard and farm. South of the stream and the path in the south valley the Black Friars had their monastery, then decorated with hangings of Edward II captured at Bannockburn. Behind the monastery garden was the church of Our Lady of St Mary-in-the-Fields. Beyond on the south and north was the forest of Drumselch, the name remaining from the Celtic period (the ridge of hunting). Outside the walls the Canongate was being built on. Merchant Guilds of merchants (who did not work with their own hands) and craftsmen were all burgesses recognised by the twelfth century Burgh Laws, their work being connected with the simple necessities of food and clothing: the craftsmen were also the beginnings of the Incorporations of Crafts of later years. From the burgesses, men who held, originally directly from the king a plot of ground, the local Goverment was chosen.

The Nor' Loch stretched from the grounds of the old St Cuthbert's Church, which now stands at the foot of Lothian Road through what is now the valley of Princes Street Gardens to beneath the North Bridge.

A contempory report by the historian Froissart gives us an impression of what Edinburgh was like in 1341 when ambassadors came to Scotland to persuade David II to invade England. Froissart, who was described as being 'by no means unfavourable to the Scots', says that in Scotland 'a man of manners, or honourable sentiments, is not easily to be found'.

He continues:

> Those of their country are like wild and savage people, shunning acquaintance with strangers, envious of the honour or profit of every one beside themselves, and perpetually jealous of losing the mean things they have; that hardly any of the nobility kept intercourse with the French, except the earls of Douglas and Murray; that Edinburgh, although by this time the first city in Scotland, could not accommodate the French, many of whom were obliged to seek lodgings in Dunfermline, and other towns at still greater distance; that the French knights complained grievously of their accommodation; no comfortable houses, no soft beds, no walls hung with tapestry, and that it required all the prudence of the French commander to restrain their impatience for leaving so miserable a country; that when they wanted to purchase horses from the Scots, they were charged six, nay even ten times the price for which these horses would have been sold to their fellow countrymen; that when the French sent forth their servants a foraging, the Scots would lie in wait for them, plunder them of what they had gathered, beat, nay even murder them; that they could find neither saddles, bridles, nor leather to make harness, nor iron to shoe their horses, for that the Scots got all such articles ready-made from Flanders.

WEIGH-HOUSE

Shortly after the French visit, King David conferred on the burgh a piece of ground at the head of the West Bow, and a weigh-house was built. The Bow was the original entrance to Edinburgh from the west and marked the end of the Castlehill and the beginning of the Lawn (originally Land) market, now both part of what is called the Royal Mile, which also includes the High Street, Canongate and the Abbey Strand.

The weigh-house at the top of the Lawnmarket was not only a familiar building, it was essential for merchants and traders. For years it was the

standard place of weights and was 'resorted to in all cases of dispute'.

The original weigh-house on the ground granted by David II in 1352 was demolished by the English in 1381. Over the centuries it was rebuilt on at least four occasions.

After the first building, its successor, known as the Over Tron or Butter Tron, seems to have lasted till 1614 when the Council built another, which was called the Weigh-house. They ordered that all cheese and butter and other country produce and all merchandise weighing more than two pounds should be weighed there. The new building had a tower and clock. Its end came in 1650 during the Castle siege on the orders of Oliver Cromwell, leading the English army.

'Considering that the Wey-house of Edinburgh was ane great impediment to the Scottis of the Castell, the samyn being biggit on the hie calsey; thairfoir, to remove that impediment, General Cromwell gaif ordouris for demolishing of the Wey-house; and upone the last day of December 1650, the Englisches began the work, and tuik doun the stepill of it that day, and so continued till it was raised,' says the diarist John Nicoll.

Almost ten years later, in August 1660, a new weigh-house was built 'but much inferior to the former condition'. The spire and clock were removed a few years later. In the 18th century the then buzz word 'encumberance' was directed against this building, particularly as it restricted the approach to the Castle up the narrow and steep Castlehill. The state visit of George IV to the city in 1822 ensured its generally unlamented demise, and in a little footnote a contemporary writer wryly records: 'The few emblems that distinguished this homely piece of architecture were lost in the short transit from the Castlehill to the Council Chambers, having doubtless been arrested in their progress by some keen antiquarian.'

Hard by was the West Bow, the name given to the zig-lane which originally provided the western entrance into the town, the 'bow' indicating an arch which presupposes there was a gate at one time through some sort of defensive wall here, or perhaps the through-way between ancient houses into the Lawnmarket from the ascending lane on the south side.

The entrances to Edinburgh came to be known as ports – gateways in the high walls which were built at various times and which were so familiar and

The Castlehill houses which survived into the 19th and early 20th centuries were among the oldest in the town. Historian Sir Daniel Wilson says there were 'many remarkable and once patrician alleys and mansions' before the changes wrought on the street, which was the approach to the open ground in front of the castle before the esplanade was formed.

reassuring to the inhabitants, who felt a sense of security behind their imposing bulwarks.

As the town spread rapidly in the 16th century, it outgrew the bounds of the earliest authenticated wall, that of 1450 authorised by James II in granting a licence to the Provost and Town Council to 'fosse, bulwark, wall, toure, turate, and utherwais to strengthen oure foresaid burgh in quhat maner of wise or degree that beis sene maste spedeful to thame'. This was all in view of the possible danger from 'oure enemies of England'.

Like so many things in Edinburgh, however, it took time to complete, and more than 20 years later it was still not finished. While the burgesses might want the safety of a town wall, they seemed unwilling to meet the costs, and the king had to lay down the regal law and instruct the Sheriff and Provost to raise the money compulsorily.

This King's Wall, as it is known, started from the Castle outer wall and continued eastward by the line of the present-day Johnston Terrace about half-way up the slope between the High Street and the Cowgate to around South Gray's Close, and then across the foot of the High Street.

The Lawnmarket – originally called the Landmarket, where produce from the country fields was sold – was lined by the typical high Edinburgh tenements. The buildings gradually extended outwards onto the road space, many of them projecting over arched arcades.

A second wall in the 16th century, the Flodden Wall, followed the disaster on that battlefield in 1513 when the Scottish king and his army were slaughtered. Again the town feared invasion by the English after the battle, and shortly after the catastrophic defeat the magistrates decided to bolster the defences. Many of the town's dwellings were now well outside the King's Wall, and while it was the custom for houses and gardens to be strengthened as bulwarks, the need for a proper defence was again deemed essential.

But again it was going to be an expensive business, with much more land having to be enclosed. It would protect the Grassmarket and Cowgate suburbs, and the Kirk o' Field, Greyfriars and Blackfriars Priories. Already there appeared to be gates named Kirk o' Field Port and West Port (at the western end of the Grassmarket), indicating that an extension to the walls was at least being planned before Flodden gave a renewed urgency.

Expediency weighed against cost, however, and as late as 1560 the wall seems not to have been fully finished. Its route can still be traced although much of the structure itself and the old ports are inevitably lost. Starting from the Half-Moon Battery at the Castle, the Flodden Wall ran south to the

Grassmarket by the western end of what was the married soldiers' quarters in Johnston Terrace (the building is now a hostel for homeless people and a plaque records the site of the King's Wall). At the south-west corner of the Grassmarket stood the West Port.

West Port

The name still survives, although there is no trace of the gateway or its stanchions now. Like the other gates, it often displayed the heads of those who had been executed for some offence or other, frequently political and sometimes for murder or theft. Or perhaps simply victims of the town's pretty rough justice of the time.

Skulls were displayed on spikes above the gate and other limbs or entire bodies were suspended to dangle in the raw winter winds or putrefy in the summer sun. Just a gentle reminder to behave yourself in the good town of Edinburgh!

On one occasion in 1681, two heads which had been mounted in the West Port were 'stollen away'. The order was given that, as three Covenanters were to be hanged in the Grassmarket, the heads of two of those executed should be struck off and used as replacements for the port's decoration.

In happier times, this gateway was the site of joyous receptions for monarchs visting Edinburgh. When King James VI returned in 1617 to his native city for the first time since inheriting the throne of Britain, 14 years earlier, he received a tumultous and expensive welcome through the ornately decorated port. A costumed figure called the Nymph Edina was on hand to greet his son Charles 1 in 1633 with an oration and, accompanied by a retinue of 'beautiful damsels', made the traditional presention to the king of the keys of the city. Charles had to endure on that occasion a further 'copious speech' from the Lady Caledonia when he turned into the West Bow.

The Flodden Wall rose up the east side of the Vennel, now stepped to the top, where a tower still stands. It then ran along what is now the north side of George Heriot's School and the west and south sides of the old Greyfriars Monastery garden. Another fortified gateway, known variously as the Society,

OPPOSITE.
Bristo Port was one of the gates into the old city. Travellers from the south passed beneath the archway which stood close to the Charity Workshop and the Bedlam. The gate is remembered in the short street carrying its name today.

M. MUNRO. CAP MAKER

Greyfriars and the Bristo Port, stood there to give access from the southern approaches.

BRISTO PORT

The Bristo, or Bristow, Port was built around 1515 as part of the decision to extend the walls after Flodden. It was at the head of Candlemaker Row, close to the grounds of Greyfriars Monastery (later the site of Greyfriars Kirk and the city's graveyard) and near to the neighbourhood occupied later in the 16th century by the Society of Brewers, hence the various names given to the old port.

The wall continued more or less along the line of the Royal Scottish Museum in present-day Chambers Street to West College Street, where there was another gate – Potterrow Port, St Mary's-in-the-Field Port or Kirk o'Field Port were its names. A significant section of the Flodden Wall still remains after its turn from the line of Drummond Street and down the Pleasance to the Cowgate.

COWGATE PORT

At the eastern end of the Cowgate, the second street in the medieval town, stood the Cowgate Port, at the foot of St Mary's Wynd. Also known as the Blackfriars' Port, after the nearby monastery, it opened originally on to the countryside and latterly to the South Back of the Canongate, the separate burgh which lay outside the town proper. The port was constructed as part of the extended wall started after Flodden. Some time later another port was built across St Mary's Wynd at its junction with the Pleasance, bearing the name St Mary's, or Pleasance, Port.

From this latter gate also were frequently displayed dismembered limbs of political prisoners, such as those Covenanters whose heads were ordered 'to be struck off, and set upon pricks upon the Pleasance Port of Edinburgh'.

On the approach of the Jacobite rebels in 1715, it was taken down because it was judged too difficult to defend. Part of the wall remained, however,

OPPOSITE.
The Cowgate Port stood at the eastern end of the Old Town's second street, opening originally onto the countryside and allowing cattle to be led by the drovers to their grazing grounds.

topped by one of the grisly iron spikes which bore the skulls of earlier times, until that was demolished in 1837.

The town defence ran up the west side of St Mary's Wynd, where house-holders were ordered to raise their garden walls and bolster their house gables to make a suitable barrier against possible intruders, to the wynd's junction with the foot of the High Street, where stood the impressive Nether Bow Port, perhaps in its later form the most attractive of all the city gates.

The Flodden Wall probably linked with remnants of the King's Wall hereabouts and continued along Leith Wynd, eventually running to the corner of the Nor' Loch and the gate at the foot of Halkerston's Wynd, named New Port. The northern defence of the town was deemed to be safe from that point because of the Nor' Loch itself.

Final additions to the town wall came between 1628 and 1636, when George Heriot's Hospital and further land south of Greyfriars Churchyard were incorpated behind the Telfer Wall. Portions of that wall can still be seen at the top of the Vennel, where the Flodden Wall tower still stands, and in Lauriston Place. Other remains of the Flodden Wall are in Greyfriars Churchyard, and in Forrest Road a narrow space between two later tenements is filled with a slice of the wall.

After the final collapse of the Jacobite cause at Culloden in 1746, there was little likelihood of further major civil strife or threat of invasion in Edinburgh, and the town wall came to be seen as an encumbrance at a time when there was talk of the town having to expand out of its existing very tight royalty. The narrow ports in particular restricted the flow of traffic and caused congestion.

They were also regarded by outsiders in the 18th century as restrictions on free trade in the town. A pamphlet in 1764 by a 'Merchant Citizen' protests at the delays at the gates when incoming traders were stopped and searched for possible smuggled goods. The pamphlet dictates that 'they altogether decline to deal with the merchant shopkeepers of Edinburgh because there is a wall surrounding the city and the Revenue officers and waiters stationed at all the Gate and Entries of the city night and day ... to stop, detain and seize their goods at their pleasure, which is not done in any city, town or corporation in all Britain.'

OPPOSITE.
The Nether Bow Port at the foot of the High Street was the most magnificent of all the city's old gateways. Its demolition in 1764 was bitterly opposed, but the narrowness of the entryway and its position meant that it was regarded as a traffic hazard. The clock is now on the Dean Gallery at Belford.

NETHER BOW PORT

That same year, the Nether Bow Port was taken down to allow free access from the High Street into the Canongate and to the road to Leith. In 1787, most of the other gateways were finally removed, and in the first half of the 19th century the city walls all but vanished, many of the stones finding their way into other buildings or gardens.

The demolition of the Nether Bow Port in 1764 came after earlier protests about a proposal to sweep it away in 1737, as a punishment by the Government following the infamous Porteous Riot of the previous year.

John Porteous, Captain of the Town Guard, had been involved in the shooting of several people at the Grassmarket execution of a smuggler, Andrew Wilson, earlier that year. For his part in the affray, Porteous was charged and convicted of murder and was incarcerated in the condemned cell in the Old Tolbooth. Word came from London of a stay of execution with a likely full reprieve to follow.

A mob was raised – it is said that some of the ringleaders were disguised in women's clothing. The crowd seized the city gates, kicked in the door of the Tolboth and marched Porteous up the Lawnmarket and down the West Bow to the Grassmarket, where he was lynched on a dyer's pole.

The Nether Bow Port was a 'handsome structure,' as historian Sir Daniel Wilson affirms in his *Memorials*,

rebuilt in its latest form in 1606, nearly in a line with St Mary's and Leith Wynds, and almost 50 yards farther eastward than the older erection. It was by far the most conspicuous and important of the six gates which gave access to the ancient capital and was regarded as an object in the maintenance and protection of which the honour of the city was so deeply involved, that, as we have seen, its demolition was one of the penalties which the Goverment sought to revenge the slight put upon the royal prerogative by the Porteous Mob.

In style of architecture it bore considerable resemblance to the ancient Porte St Honore of Paris, as represented in old engravings; and it was most probably constructed in imitation of some of the old gates of that capital, between which and Edinburgh so constant an intercourse was maintained at a somewhat earlier period.

When the destruction of this, the main port of the city was averted by the strenuous patriotic exertions of the Scottish peers and Members of Parliament, it was regarded as a national triumph; but, unhappily, towards the middle of the last century (18th), a mania siezed civic rulers throughout the kingdom for *sweeping away all the old rubbish*, as the ancient fabrics which adorned the principal towns were contemptuously styled.

The common Council of London set the example by obtaining an Act of Parliament in 1760 to remove their city gates; and, only four years afterwards, the Town Council of Edinburgh demolished the Nether Bow, one of the chief ornaments of the city, which had it been preserved, would have been now regarded as a peculiarly interesting relic of the olden town.

The building contained a number of apartments, and there was also a blacksmith's. The Nether Bow coffee house is described as being 'at the gate' and no visitor was likely to enter the town unnoticed or uncommented upon through this main portal.

Not all the Nether Bow Port is lost, however; its clock was taken to the old Orphan Hospital, and when that was demolished in 1845 it was placed on the Dean Orphanage building at Belford. That orphanage is now the Dean Gallery, and the old clock still keeps splendid time. The Nether Bow bell was also kept safely and was placed in the Church of Scotland's Netherbow Centre.

The outline of the old port is shown in brass bricks at the spot where it stood at the High Street junction with the present St Mary's and Jeffrey Streets.

The pulling down of the Nether Bow was lamented by many, not least by the poet Claudero, a somewhat eccentric character of the time whose real name was James Wilson. A native of Cumbernauld, he lived in Edinburgh for more than 30 years and was renowned as a pamphleteer as well as a satirical poet.

A sermon, preached by Claudero, on the 'Condemnation of the Nether Bow Porch of Edinburgh, 9th July, 1764', before a crowded audience, 'gave opportunity for his sarcastic wit to flow', according to one account.

What was too hard for the great ones of the earth, yea even queens, to effect, is now, even now in our day recited,' he expounded. 'No patriot duke opposed the scheme, as did the great Argyll in the great senate of our nation; therefore the project shall go into execution, and down shall Edina's lofty porches be hurled with a vengance. Streets shall be extended to the east and west, regular and beautiful ...

Our gates must be extended wide for accommodating the gilded chariots, which, from the luxury of the age, are becoming numerous. With an impetuous career they jostle against one another in our

The Old Tolbooth stood outside St Giles' and was one of the most distinctive buildings in the town. Its demolition in 1817 along with the adjoining Luckenbooths was deemed essential to opening up the High Street, which had been narrowed to something like 15 feet wide by that time. The Tolbooth's long history included its use as a meeting place for the Town Council, for the courts and for the Scots Parliament. It was also a miserable jail in which men and women passed their final days before execution. From 1785 hangings were carried out on the platform of the Tolbooth and many, including Deacon William Brodie, met their fate there.

streets, and the unwary foot passenger is in danger of being crushed to pieces. The loaded cart itself cannot withstand their fury, and the hideous yells of Coal Johnie resound through the vaulted sky. The sour milk barrels are overturned, and deluges of Corstorphin cream run down our strands, while the poor unhappy milk-maid wrings her hands with sorrow.

Who then can blame the wise guardians of Edina, whose greatest care is the preservation of her people, and the safety of her inhabitants? Blush, therefore, ye malevolant tongues, let sedition perish, and animosities be forgotten.

OLD TOLBOOTH

Another building of reassurance in Edinburgh was unquestionably the formidable slab of the Old Tolbooth which stood solidly, yet for some menacingly, in the High Street on the north-west corner of St Giles' Church. Its fearsome reputation came from its use as a place where the condemned were held to await their fate at one of the town's execution spots – the Mercat Cross, Castlehill and the Grassmarket. By 1785, when a two-storey extension had been built to enable executions to take place at the Tolbooth itself, its menace was all the more apparent and its internal arrangements were abominable to modern feelings, as many of those who were condemned to suffer as debtors found when they were cast into its unsavoury stench.

The Old Tolbooth had its roots in the first bellhous, or praetorium, which was on the south-east corner of St Giles'. This was effectively the Town House, where tolls were taken for the leasing of booths in the market places, and where the first citizen, then probably called the alderman, and the merchants would set out rules and regulations. That building, also described as a tolbooth, taxing office or taxhouse, was in existence about 1145 in the reign of David I.

The building which became known as the Old Tolbooth was erected on land gifted to the town in 1386. In his 'Charter of the site of the Bellhous', Robert II gave, granted and confirmed to the Burgesses and Community of the Burgh of Edinburgh and their successors in time to come 'sixty feet in length and thirty feet in breadth of land lying in the market place of the said burgh, on the north side of the street thereof ... to construct and erect houses and buildings on the forsaid land for the ornament of the said burgh and for their necessary use.'

There is reference to the praetorium in 1369, possibly replacing the building of King David's time, but more than likely it perished along with so much else when Edinburgh was burned to the ground by the English in 1385. Basically, the only thing left standing, it appears, was part of St Giles' Church, so King Robert's charter for a new bellhous was part of the essential replanning and rebuilding of the town.

The Tolbooth was then formed at the north-west corner of the church, the market place referred to being the square in front of St Giles' west façade. Subsequently the square was encroached upon by the extension of the line of the Lawnmarket and the extension of other buildings.

After 1482, the Bellhous title was generally replaced by Tolbooth, and one of the last mentions of Bellhous as distinct from Tolbooth, is in 1509 in an order from James IV to the Provost concerning the sale of a shop in the Bellhous to a goldsmith.

Over the centuries, various extensions and repairs were carried out to the Tolbooth until it became a substantial four- or five-storey block with many uses.

In its day it served as the market house and the Town Council meeting place. It gave accommodation to various courts including the Court of Session after its inauguration in 1532, and housed the Convention of Royal Burghs. The Scottish Parliament also met there. As far back as 1480, its use as a prison is recorded, and when some rebuilding of a section which had become dangerous was required in 1554, the work was noted as being for 'the new Prison Hous'. This was later known as the Thieves' Hole, although that section of the building in its final years was a shoe shop.

In some respects the Tolbooth was lucky to survive as long as it did. In 1561 it came under royal scrutiny when it was described as being in a 'very ruinous state'. The Privy Council sent a letter to the Town Council expressing Queen Mary's concern that the building was likely 'haistillie to dekay and fall down'. She ordered the Provost, Baillies and Council 'to caus put workmen to the taking down of the said tolbooth with all possible diligence'.

Whether Queen Mary's instructions to demolish and rebuild were carried out to the letter is open to doubt – it was certainly reconstructed and extended. Under threat of the Lords of Session removing their court to St Andrews, the Town Council ordered the construction of what was called the New Tolbooth, close to the south-west corner of St Giles'. There the Council and Lords of Session – and occasionally the members of the Scots Parliament – gathered. From 1564 until 1811 the New Tolbooth served as a meeting place. The building appears to have been three storeys high, starkly utilitarian and with no great architectural attractions, and its demolition in 1811–12 caused little comment.

The Old Tolbooth, however, continued to play an important role in the town's life. After the rehousing of the principal courts in Parliament House in 1640, it became primarily the city's jail.

The Edinburgh historian Hugo Arnot gives us a fine, if gruesome, description of the building the author Sir Walter Scott was to christen 'The Heart of Midlothian'.

The ground floor was, says Arnot in 1779, let out as as shops and cut off from the rest of the premises. 'The three stories above are all places of restraint, destined for the wretched.'

Many of those 'wretched' by that time were debtors, incarcerated until family or friends could raise the money to settle outstanding dues, and there was still a condemned cell where those awaiting execution were held.

Of conditions in the Old Tolbooth, Arnot relates: 'In the heart of a great city it is not accommodated with ventilation, with water-pipes, with privy. The filth collected in the jail is thrown into a hole within the house, at the foot of the stair, which, it is pretended, communicates with a drain: but, if so, it is completely choked, as to serve no other purpose but that filling the jail with disagreeable stench.' He continues:

When we visited the jail there were confined in it about twenty-nine prisoners partly debtors, partly delinquents; four or five were women, and there were five boys. Some of these had what is called the freedom of the prison, that is, not being confined to a single apartment. As these people had the liberty of going up and down the stairs, they kept their rooms tolerably cleanly swept. They had beds belonging to themselves, and in one room we observed a pot upon the fire. But, wherever we found the prisoners confined to one apartment, whether on account of their delinquencies, or what they were unable to pay for a little freedom, the rooms were all destitute of all accommodation, and were very nasty.

All parts of the jail were kept in a slovenly condition; But the eastern quarter of it (although we had fortified ourselves against the stench) was intolerable. This consisted of three apartments, each above the other. In what length of time these rooms, and the stairs leading up to them, could have collected the quantity of filth which we saw in them, we cannot determine. The undermost of these apartments was empty. In the second, which is called the iron room, which is destined for those who have received the sentence of death, there were three boys: one of them might have been fourteen, the others about twelve years of age. They had been confined about three weeks for thievish practices. In the corner of the room, we saw shoved together a quantity of dust, rags and straw, the refuse of a long succession of criminals. The straw had originally been put in the room for them to lie upon, but had been suffered to remain, till, worn by successive convicts, it was chopped into bits of two inches long. From this we went to an apartment above, were there two miserable boys, not twelve years of age. But there we had no leisure for observation; for, no sooner was the door opened, than such an insufferable stench assailed us, from the stagnant and putrid air of the room, as, not withstanding our precautions, utterly overwhelmed us.

Nothing, wrote the young sensitive advocate historian, could be more inhuman than such treatment of the prisoners.

The Old Tolbooth extended out into the High Street and by 1817, with a new prison built on the Calton Hill, it was regarded as yet another 'encumbrance' as it impeded free access up the High Street to the Lawnmarket. It was simply pulled down, with some of its stone incorporated, it is said, into sewer and drainage work in the New Town and into a tenement in Leith. The door from the condemned cell found its way to Abbotsford, the Borders home of Sir Walter Scott, who one way or another acquired a fine collection of Edinburgh curiosities. The place of public execution was moved to the head of Libberton's Wynd.

Today the site of the Old Tolbooth is marked in granite setts in the shape of a heart – Scott's 'Heart of Midlothian' – in the High Street. For whatever reason, spitting on the heart became a local custom, which continues to this day.

LUCKENBOOTHS

Writing at the time of the Old Tolbooth's demolition, Scott describes the building:

> The prison reared it ancient front in the very middle of the High Street, forming the termination to a huge pile of buildings called the Luckenbooths, which, for some inconceivable reason, our ancestors had jammed into the midst of the principal street of the town, leaving for passage a narrow way on the north; and on the south, into which the prison opens, a crooked lane, winding betwixt the high and sombre walls of the Tolbooth and the adjacent houses on the one side, and the buttresses and projections of the old cathedral upon the other.
>
> To give some gaiety to this sombre passage, well known by the name of the Krames, a number of little booths, or shops, after the fashion of cobbler's stalls, were plastered, as it were, against the Gothic projections and abutments (of St Giles').

The Luckenbooths (or locking-up shops) were a picturesque block of houses and shops at the eastern end of the Old Tolbooth, and among the famous Edinburgh citizens who did their business there was Allan Ramsay, the poet.

OPPOSITE.
The High Street, the extension of the Lawnmarket seen here eastwards, was the centre of life for the old town. At one time it teemed with markets and the cries of the hucksters filled the air, while human and animal waste polluted the earthen roadway.

Among his many accomplishments, he was a publisher, and Ramsay's shop became the gathering place for the literati in the 18th century. From there, he launched the country's first circulating library in 1725.

The shop below was later occupied by William Creech, another publisher, who produced the Edinburgh edition of Robert Burns' poems, and went on the become a Lord Provost.

THE KRAMES

Between the Luckenbooths and the walls of St Giles' was the narrow lane Scott described, where the travelling pedlars and small traders set up their stalls. In the narrowness and bustle of the place, shoppers would seek out the bargains.

The Krames also attracted the boyhood attention of the Scottish judge Lord Cockburn. The 'delightful place' was used by 'shopless traffickers' from about 1550:

> In my boyhood their little stands, each enclosed in a tiny room of its own, and during the day all open to the little footpath that ran between the two rows of them, all glittering with attractions, contained everthing fascinating to childhood, but chiefly toys. It was like one of the Arabian Nights bazaars in Baghdad. Throughout the whole year it was an enchantment. Let anyone fancy what it was about the New Year, when every child had got its handsel, and every farthing of every handsel was spent there. The Krames was the paradise of childhood.

That paradise went, along with the Tolbooth and the Luckenbooths, in 1817.

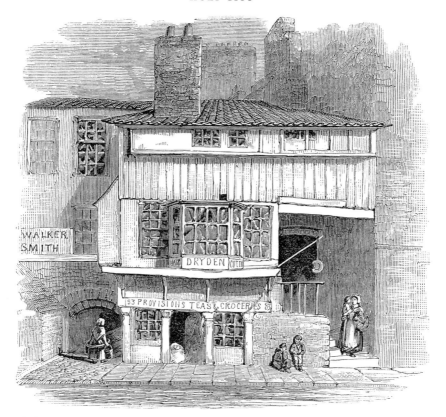

The houses in the Cowgate were at one time deemed the best address in Edinburgh and many distinguished citizens lived there. They gained access to the High Street by climbing the steep closes and wynds which linked the two streets.

only through north and south traffic was outside the city wall. Wynds ran down the slopes to the valley and up again the other side. Gardens were being built on,' says MacRae. He continues:

> The ceremonial approach was by the West Port through the Grassmarket and up the West Bow, the Upper Bow having a gradient of one in five. Most of the houses had still thatched roofs.
> The jousting ground at the Barras, west of the Grassmarket, laid out by the English occupiers some two and a quarter centuries before, with its attendant chapel, was still complete but no longer used for tournaments. The later tournament ground of Greenside adjoining the church of the Carmelite Friars was being used for open air plays.
> Two miles out in the forest to the south was a hospital for segregation and treatment during the plague adjoining the Chapel of

The Canongate, which is the lower section of the Royal Mile, as it looked in 1829. On the left is the gate of one of the distinguished properties no longer there – John Adam's Milton House of 1755. Four large 1758 landscape panels by William Delacour which were removed from the house are incorporated into Milton House School.

St Roque, 'patron of pestilences,' whose cemetery was used along with local temporary cleansing stations on each outbreak.

Inhabitants were reminded of justice by the branks at the Mercat Cross and the stocks at the Canongate Tolbooth, while grisly heads could be seen 'upon a prick at the highest stone of the Gavell of the Tolbooth towards the publik street'.

The cross of St John stood in the street at the head of the Canongate. The Canongate had its own cross and at the foot of the street was the Girth Cross, which had to be touched by those who fled from justice at the boundary of the sanctuary of the Holyrood Abbey precincts.

Along the Water of Leith a mile away was a chain of water-driven mills with little communities growing around them, at this time chiefly for grinding meal for the burgh. Many of those mills were already several hundreds of years old.

It was around this time that a major change took place in the shape of Edinburgh with the arrival of the Protestant Reformation in what had been a Roman Catholic country. The destruction of ecclestiastical buildings brought untold damage and desecration. All the religious houses, including St Giles' Kirk, suffered in those tumultuous days of 1559. It was recorded by a diarist quoted by the Rev. Dr J. Cameron Lees in his history of St Giles:

> Upon the 14th day of July in the year of God abon rehersit, the Blak and Gray Freris of Edinburgh were demolished and casten down aluterlie, and all the chepellis and collegis about the said burgh with thair yairds were in likewise destroyit, and the images and altaris of Sanct Giles kirk destroyit and brint.

BLACK FRIARS' MONASTERY

Founded by Alexander II in 1230, the monastery of the Black Friars (or Dominicans) stood in extensive grounds to the south of the Cowgate and, with the neighbouring collegiate church of St Mary's-in-the-Field (better known as Kirk o' Field), the combined area of the ecclesiastical ground stretched between the Pleasance and the Potterrow.

The monastery stood pretty much on the site of the old High School at the foot of the present Infirmary Street. Kirk o' Field was in part on the site of today's University Old College at South Bridge.

The monastery was originally known as the Mansio Regis, as King Alexander had a house there. From its start it appears to have been a wealthy foundation – its church had a central rood-tower and high spire – enlarged by benefactions from Robert I and James III. It was accidentally destroyed by fire in 1528, but it is speculated that the church itself was only partially damaged. Further harm may have been done in the 1544 English invasion, but its destruction came at the time of the Reformation when, in 1559, the complex of church, cloister, and domestic buildings was looted and ravaged. The garden and cemetery are also unlikely to have escaped the attention of the attackers.

Blackfriars' Wynd, which took its name from the Dominican order and ran into the Cowgate, was the direct access from the High Street. The narrow alley was also the monks' property, having been endowed by Alexander. At the corner of the wynd and the Cowgate was the episcopal house or palace of the Archbishop of St Andrews.

John Knox, one of the great Protestant figures in Scotland, was summoned to an ecclesiastical judicatory in the Blackfriars church in 1556 for preaching against the 'idolatory' mass, but the case was not proceeded with for fear of stirring up trouble amongst the townsfolk, and possibly further afield.

KIRK O' FIELD

When first built, probably around the same time as the Dominican monastery, the Kirk o' Field was on a commanding position to the south of the town and outside its walls. It was finally enclosed by the Flodden Wall.

In a view of the town in 1544, it appears as a large cross church with a central tower – a 'large and handsome building' it is called. Under the dependence of Holyrood Abbey, with the growing importance of the Cowgate the church was elevated to collegiate status early in the 16th century and a provost appointed.

It, too, fell to the Reformers' onslaught.

In its grounds in the Old Provost's House, Lord Darnley, husband of Mary, Queen of Scots, was murdered in mysterious circumstances in 1567 and that is what elevates it into a special place in Edinburgh's history.

'The history of the Collegiate Church of St Mary's-in-the-Field presents scarcely any other feature of interest than that which attaches to it as the scene of so strange and memorable a tragedy,' comments Wilson.

On the site of the church's hospital, also destroyed by the English in 1544, the Duke of Chatelherault built a mansion which later became the library for the University before being demolished in 1798.

GREY FRIARS' MONASTERY

The monastery of the Franciscans or Grey Friars (so called because of the colour of their habits, as were the Black Friars) was founded at the behest of James I for the encouragement of learning.

The building on the south side of the Grassmarket was so magnificent that when the first brothers of the order, founded by St Francis of Assisi, came to Edinburgh around 1447, ten years after the death of James I, they were overwhelmed by the grandeur of their friary and the adjoining garden lands. They had been sent to the cold Scottish town by the Vice-General of Cologne

OPPOSITE.
The names of the closes and wynds were often self-evident. They were named after the person who had the biggest or most important property there, or indicated a specific association. Blackfriars' Wynd was so named because it was the principal route from the High Street to the priory of the Black Friars on the south side of the Cowgate.

in response to the king's request, but it seems that the designated prior, Cornelius of Zurich, a distinguished scholar, had to be persuaded by the Bishop of St Andrews over a period of years to take up residence – after all, the order was created to serve the poor.

The Grey Friars may have been accustomed to much humbler accommodation, but the comfortable lodgings in Edinburgh were appreciated by Mary of Gueldres in 1449, when she arrived for her marriage to James II. Another royal visitor was Henry VI of England, who found refuge in the friary after he was forced to flee to Scotland.

In 1559, which brought 'the bursting of the storm of the Reformation', as Dr Lees puts it, the monastery, like other religious buildings, was attacked, pillaged and left in ruins. On its dissolution, the Grey Friars fled to the Netherlands.

Stones from the ruins, and from the Black Friars' premises, were used for building dykes and other work by the Council. But it was not long before the Grey Friars' ground was to have a new purpose altogether. The Council approached Queen Mary with a request to use the garden area 'being sumquhat distant fra oure toun' as a public burial ground. Royal sanction was given in 1562 and within a fortnight, it is said, it was in use as a cemetery. It replaced the old graveyard to the south of St Giles' on the land descending to the Cowgate. When a virulent plague swept through Edinburgh in 1568, a huge pit to receive the dead was ordered to be dug in the new graveyard.

The original entrance to Greyfriars yard is at the north end, at the foot of Candlemaker Row, and dates to the 1562 acquisition.

The Greyfriars Church opened in 1620, when worshippers at first sat on stools. It was used by the Town Council as a gunpowder store and in 1718 an explosion seriously damaged the original church tower and adjoining west gable. The church was repaired, but the Council decided to take away the tower and build another church adjoining the first.

The Old Greyfriars Church was destroyed by fire in 1845, and the building restored. The congregations of Old and New Greyfriars continued to worship separately until finally being united in 1929.

Among the other requests made by the Council in the petition to Queen Mary was that the ground belonging to the Black Friars lying between the Cowgate and the city wall should be passsed to them to build a hospital for the poor, and that the Kirk o' Field and its adjoining buildings and ground should be used for a public school. The queen, while accepting almost at once the Grey Friars land plan, held out until 1566 before ceding the other ground, arguing that once the Council came up with the money for the hospital and school she would provide suitable sites.

Maison Dieu

To the east of the Grey Friars monastery was a small hospital called Maison Dieu, a name applied to several such places in the town. But at the beginning of the 16th century it had become ruinous, according to Arnot. Effectively, it was replaced by the foundation of the Chapel and Hospital of St Mary Magdalene in the Cowgate. The Magdalene Chapel is one of the most prized buildings in the city today, and owes its continued existence to its 16th-century patrons, the Incorporation of Hammermen, who changed at the Reformation to the new form of worship, thus saving it from the prevailing desecration.

Much was lost in Edinburgh in those days of religious fervour which swept through Scotland, and many of the churches which were not destroyed were stripped of rich decoration and stained glass. Now the only pre-Reformation stained glass in Scotland is in the Magdalene Chapel in the Cowgate. MacRae says of the period ending in 1560 that not many buildings survived except parts of the Castle, the ruined nave of Holyrood Abbey (also targeted by the mobs) and the north-west portion of the Trinity College Church and its altar-piece diptych dating from 1470 (now on display in the National Gallery at the Mound).

Trinity College Church was a 15th-century foundation by Mary of Gueldres,
the wife of James II, together with the associated Trinity Hospital. Only the choir and transept
of the church were completed, and the nave Mary wished it to have was never built.

Trinity College Church would survive for almost three centuries further, but meet an unhappy end, as we shall see.

Of the land eventually taken from the Queen? The Council successfully requested a charter from her son, James VI indemnifying them for not building a hospital, and struck an agreement that if they disposed of the land the money raised and feus would go towards the endowment of a hospital at Trinity College Church.

On the largest site of the Black Friars, a High School was formed in 1578; Lady Yester's Church was built in 1635; the Surgeons' Hall in 1697 and in 1738 the Royal Infirmary was started. On the Kirk o' Field site, the University, or 'tounis colledge', was formed. There was no question of valuable land in a burgeoning burgh being left fallow.

Many other religious houses, some of which provided shelter and treatment for the poor, flourished over the centuries, but have vanished from our eyes.

CHAPEL OF HOLY RUDE

This was founded in 1528 by Walter Chepman, the man given royal warrant in 1507 to open Scotland's first printing press in the Cowgate. It was a tribute to his late and present wives and 'for all of both sexes whose bodies are buried within the church of St Giles'.

He also laid down the 'usual regulation regarding the chaplain who would oversee the chapel'. These were:

> If the said chaplain keep a whore in his house, or engages in games of cards or dice, or similar games, he shall lose his chaplaincy; also, if he does not continuously celebrate mass within the chapel for twenty days, he is to have no right to church women, baptise, marry or bury without the consent of the Provost of St Giles' and Prependaries, and if he attempts to do any such things without licence from the mother church, he shall lose his chaplaincy.

The chapel stood on the lower part of the old church yard of St Giles', on the land tumbling down in terraces to the Cowgate. It seems to have disappeared by the end of the 16th century, and Wilson suggests the chapel might have gone just post-Reformation, with its stones being used for building the New Tolbooth close to St Giles' itself.

With the acquisition of the Grey Friars' land for a cemetery, the ground to the south of St Giles' was abandoned as a churchyard, and in due course it came to be covered over by the Parliament House complex of courts.

'Instead of some old monk or priest treading among its grassy hillocks (of the open churchyard) it became the lounge of grooms and lackeys waiting on their masters during the meetings of Parliament, or of quarrelsome litigants, and the usual retainers of the law, during the sessions of the College of Justice; all idea of sacredness must have been lost,' Wilson observes.

BELL'S WYND – MAISON DIEU

Another chapel, also called Maison Dieu, which was altered by the Reformation events, stood at the head of Bell's Wynd in the High Street. The building fell into private hands.

ST MARY'S CHAPEL

In the middle of Niddry's Wynd, another of the links between the High Street and the Cowgate, was St Mary's Chapel, founded and endowed in 1504. In 1618 it passed into the possession of the Incorporation of Wrights and Masons and was used as their meeting place before new premises were built when the wynd was swept away by the construction of South Bridge and replaced by the present Niddry Street, slightly further to the east of the wynd's line.

At the head of St Mary's Wynd, on its west side, were a chapel and convent for Cistercian nuns and a hospital dedicated to the Virgin Mary. Its name continues in the present St Mary's Street.

Possibly the earliest recorded hospital within the old town, it was founded by the magistrates in 1438 and there is a record of its being reroofed in 1508. At least one source speculates that the chapel was in existence in the 14th century, and in 1499 the Council ordered citizens to beg for money from their fellows to support the inmates of the hospital.

ST NINIAN'S CHAPEL

Another little chapel dedicated to St Ninian rested in the lee of the Calton Crag, close to where the Regent Arch in Waterloo Place would be built. In the 18th

St Mary's Wynd was swept away in the big improvement schemes of the 19th century, designed to remove many old buildings, which were slums with people crammed into unsanitary and damp conditions. The old wynd was replaced by St Mary's Street.

A sketch showing the last remains of St Mary's Chapel in Portsburgh, just off the west end of the Grassmarket and nestling beneath the Castle rock.

century, Arnot records that it had been turned into a dwelling, and in 1778 one of its remaining relics, the baptismal font, was rescued from possible destruction by being taken into the care of the acquisitive Writer to the Signet Walter Ross, whose folly tower at Stockbridge housed many curios of the old town.

When Ross's tower at Deanhaugh was demolished in 1816, the font found its way to Abbotsford, the Borders home of that other avid collector of Edinburghalia, Sir Walter Scott.

St Thomas's Hospital

Founded in the reign of James V in 1541 by George Crichton, the Bishop of Dunkeld, this was another charitable institution with a chapel and almshouse. The almsmen were dressed in red gowns at public processions.

In 1617 it was disposed of by the chaplains and bedesmen to the bailies of the Canongate. It was still intended to be a hospital for the poor, and when it was rebuilt by the new owners a carving of figures of two cripples, a man and a woman, was placed over the entrance.

There was a scandal over the embezzlement of revenues, and the Canongate magistrates sold the hospital to the local kirk session in 1634, but in 1747 it was converted into a coach house which fell into disrepair before being pulled down in 1778.

St Mary's, Portsburgh

Another chapel dedicated to St Mary was at the foot of Chapel or Lady's Wynd, just off the West Port at the western entrance to the Grassmarket. It stood close to the barrace or tilting grounds, and probably wounded or dying combatants received bodily or spiritual succour there at one time. By the 1780s it was in ruins, although Chapel Wynd is a reminder of its existence.

St Sebastian's

Another small chapel was that of St Sebastian in Easter Portsburgh, on the grounds of Bristo. It was still there in 1591.

St Sebastian was the saint whose aid was called for to avert the pestilence, and St Roque was beseeched to cure the disease.

The ruins of St Roque's Chapel built on the old Burgh Muir, near where the
Astley Ainslie Hospital now stands. On the muir the Scottish army mustered before setting
off to the disastrous confrontation with English troops on Flodden Field.

St Roque's

The large chapel of St Roque, or St Roche, formerly stood at the west end of the old Burgh Muir, within what are now the grounds of the Astley Ainslie Hospital at Morningside.

Round it was a cemetery in which many of the townsfolk who died of the plague were buried, and it also seems likely that the ill were treated in specially erected wooden huts round the chapel and its hospital.

The Council in 1532 granted an additional four acres of ground to the chaplain Sir John Young, but after the Reformation the property and the graveyard fell into private hands. Arnot relates that in the 1750s, when the then proprietor employed masons to pull down the walls of the old chapel building, the scaffolding gave way and one man was killed. He notes:

The accident was looked upon as a judgment against those who were demolishing the church of God. No entreaties nor bribes by the proprietor could prevail upon tradesmen to accomplish the demolition.

The first mention of the chapel of St Roque is in 1507, when James IV visited it, confirming that it had most likely been in existence for some years by then. Derelict by 1789, it was finally demolished in 1791 – perhaps by less God-fearing workmen.

St Catherine's of Siena

Another chapel on the muir was that of St John the Baptist, founded in 1502 by Sir John Crawford, a canon at St Giles'. It was probably a chapel-of-ease for about five years before serving as the chapel of the nunnery of St Catherine of Siena.

The Convent of the Sisters of the Order of Friars Preachers was founded after 1513 by a group of women whose husbands or relatives had perished with their king on the battlefield of Flodden. The Scots army had gathered on the Burgh Muir before setting out on what was to be a disastrous venture.

It was on ground bounded by the present Sciennes Road (the name is a corruption of Siena), Causewayside, Grange Loan and St Catherine's Place. In a garden in the latter street, a stone from the convent is still preserved.

The convent was attacked on the eve of the Reformation and badly damaged, but not totally laid to waste. Parts of the ruins served as a plague hospital in 1645, and its 12-foot-high enclosing wall was taken down about 1760.

Near St Catherine's was a chapel of Knights Templar, who named their building Holy Mount as it stood on a rise there around the area of today's Preston Street.

St Leonard's

On the east side of Dalkeith Road were a chapel and hospital dedicated to St Leonard, giving us the area of town we call St Leonard's. It was also on higher ground, on the edge of Holyrood Park, and the site was later occupied by James Clark School, now itself converted for housing.

The hospital and chapel belonged to Holyrood Abbey and were in existence in 1271. The last remains of the chapel wall, then four feet high, were destroyed in 1854. At that time, many skeletons were found inside and outside the chapel precincts, presumably those of the inmates or patients who had died from their illnesses.

'St Mary's of Placentia'

The name of the Pleasance is commonly believed to derive from an ancient priory of nuns dedicated to St Mary of Placentia, which stood closer to the Flodden Wall, but still outside the town.

It is an urban myth. No such saint exists and there was no priory.

The authority for the priory and its name, which has passed down through the generations, is William Maitland, who wrote about it in his 1753 *History of Edinburgh*. He seems simply to have invented a picturesque background to explain the derivation of the Pleasance. The Scots word 'plesance' means a park or garden, and the name is recorded in 1507 as a house in its own grounds in the area.

Rude Chapel, Greenside

Standing on the west side of the Calton Hill, its origins are uncertain, but by the 16th century Holyrood Abbey had claimed it. The chapel may have been founded about 1456, when James II gave the town the ground of Greenside as a playing field. In the 1520s the magistrates gave the chapel to the Carmelite Friars and its last mention as a religious house seems to be in 1543. Suppressed at the Reformation, the building was put to another use around 1591 – a hospital founded by a city merchant, John Robertson, for lepers.

Paul's Work

As far back as 1479, a hospital for 'the reception and entertainment', as Arnot puts it, of 12 poor men was founded in Leith Wynd, not far from the Nether Bow Port. It was called The Hospital of our Blessed Lady and provided shelter to the deserving over the years.

The Town Council took over responsibility for the hospital after the Reformation, and when the property fell into a ruinous state it was rebuilt in 1619 and given the name Paul's Work. It became a workhouse, and five men

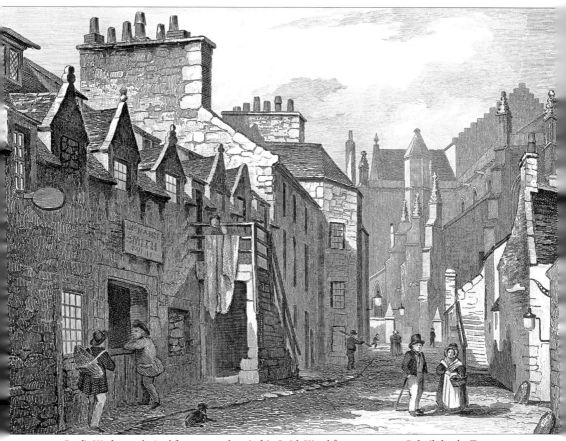

Paul's Work was derived from a 1479 hospital in Leith Wynd for 12 poor men. Rebuilt by the Town Council in the 17th century, it was named Paul's Work, and run as a workhouse for vagrant boys and girls. It later became a house of correction.

were brought from Holland to instruct vagrant boys and girls in the arts of making coarse woollen goods. This was not a successful enterprise, however, and the Council grew tired of trying to make a go of it, although the workhouse had attracted considerable donations from 'many well disposed people'.

It was turned into a house of correction, but was later sold on to a cloth manufacturer. The property was finally removed by the North British Railway Company around the middle of the 19th century.

CHAPTER 4

'THE LORD IS ANGRY'

The people of Edinburgh knew only too well how fire could destroy their homes after English excursions, but the growing town still managed many self-inflicted destructions of 16th-century buildings. In December 1585, for instance, fire broke out in Peebles Wynd (where Blair Street now runs down beside the Tron Kirk to the Cowgate).

'Citizens were greatly alarmed, and the conflagration of the whole neighbourhood for some time apprehended,' says one report. A baker's boy had apparently, either accidentally or deliberately, set fire to a stack of peats belonging to his master. It was then common practice to stack heather, broom, whins and other peats in the passageways or closes leading to the houses – 'to the great discontent of the people and the danger of the neighbourhood'. The unfortunate lad suffered the severest of punishments – he was himself burned to death at the Mercat Cross the next day. It was a salutary warning to anyone meddling with fire. Shortly after, the Town Council published an edict forbidding the piling of fuel within the city.

This latter part of the century was seeing changes in the shape of the town. Still contained in its medieval pattern within its walls, the population was increasing steadily. For some time there had been building on the garden spaces – unlike in the Canongate – behind the original houses down the slopes to the north and south from the ridge. Only a narrow path (or close) was left off the main street to provide access to the back lands. The houses on the main frontages were rebuilt as tenements or 'lands' and increases in height to eight, ten or 12 storeys were not uncommon further down the slope. Thus Edinburgh had its high buildings before the term 'skyscraper' was invented.

The new building style brought its own problems, particularly from illness, as people lived so tightly together. Plague and leprosy were frequent and the penalty for sheltering a sufferer was death.

The frequency of fires and the structural dangers of building high forced the Scots Parliament in 1624 to forbid the use of thatch for roofing – slates, tiles or lead had to be used. A further Act in 1698 stated:

> Taking into consideration the great danger the Edinburghers were exposed to by the excessive height of their houses both in respect of fire and falling, they enacted that no building to be erected in the city thereafter shall exceed five storeys in height, the front wall at the ground storey to be three feet in thickness.

Another problem with the tenement style of building where 'a house sometimes rivalled the steeples in height' was how to dispose of human and other waste from perhaps 20 or 30 families in a huge building, particularly in the High Street itself.

'The houses being so lofty, and the streets so very narrow, were, consequently, gloomy and ill ventilated,' we are told in *Annals of Edinburgh*. 'Those who dwelt in the airy regions begrudged the toil of a descent to the street, when it could be avoided,' says one writer about the 1550s. 'Hence, the whole garbage of many families was ejected from the windows with little ceremony. But woe to the stranger who ventured to go forth in the hope of inhaling the morning breeze; a whole volley of miscellaneous accumulations of abominatons might light upon his head, before the tardy warning of "get out of the way" could travel to his ears.'

Traditionally, the cry from the upper windows as the overnight chamber pots were emptied onto the close many levels below was 'Gardyloo!' from the French – 'Watch out for the water'. The Edinburgher or seasoned visitor would hurl back the desperate plea 'Haud yer hand!' to give him valuable time to avoid an unsavoury drenching by dashing up or down the close. It is something we have thankfully lost, although seeing the streets of modern Edinburgh, it seems that traditions die hard when it comes to general cleanliness and tidiness.

Other sources of dirtiness, as the *Annals* relate, were

> that every inhabitant had his own dunghill in the streets, opposite his door, and of there being so many outside stairs projecting from the houses under which swine were kept by the inhabitants, that were allowed at pleasure to wander about the streets, and play the part of scavengers.
>
> These animals naturally became the pets and play-fellows of the young people; and thus a litter of pigs and children might be seen playing lovingly together in the mud.

The Council ordered the removal of the dunghills and the swine to be prevented from 'pestering the streets'. It took many years before the pigs were finally banished. Robert Chambers, in his *Traditions*, tells the story of the girl who was to become the Duchess of Gordon riding upon a sow in the High Street, and that was in the middle of the 18th century. But although the pigs might be a tolerated nuisance, there was certainly some order in the once-congested High Street by the insistance of the king that the markets be allocated to specific streets and buildings.

The 1477 order to the Town Council saw that the market for hay, straw, grass and fodder generally was to be in the Cowgate. The salt market was in Niddry's Wynd, the fish market on both sides of the High Street above the Nether Bow with the stalls of merchants beween the Bellhouse and the Tron (weigh bar) on the north side and opposite them, on the other side of the roadway, the hatmakers and skinners. The meat market was held about the Tron and fowls were to be sold around the Mercat Cross. Meal and grain were sold from their market from the Tolbooth up to Libberton's Wynd, and beyond that, up the Lawnmarket, linen and all other cloth was sold. All butter, cheese and similar foods were allocated the Over Bow. Ironwork of all kinds was sited beneath the Nether Bow about St Mary's Wynd. Cattle were sold outside the town at the far end of the Grassmarket.

As we have seen, with Edinburgh being put to the torch in 1544, most traces of the old town apart from the Castle and St Giles' must be underground in hidden foundations and parts of the town walls which turn up in the excavation of development sites. In May 2004, for instance, what were believed to be the remains of a wall and part of the foundations of a 15th-century house were discovered on a building site in the Cowgate, throwing further light on the construction of the medieval town.

In 1600 the Duke of Rohan, writing about a visit to Edinburgh on his travels, describes the city as being 'about 1,000 paces in length and from 400–500 in breadth. There was nothing remarkable in it but the great street, which was very long and broad, extended from one end of the town to the other; the houses were not sumptious, being almost all built of wood.' As already mentioned, however, pressure was beginning to be put on the garden spaces for building and thoughts were rising higher.

The departure of James VI to claim the united throne of Britain in 1603 was marked by his granting to Edinburgh the Golden Charter, which set out clearly the area to which the royal burgh held a monopoly of trade. The boundaries extended from the edge of Edgebucking Brae, at the east end of Musselburgh links, on the east, to the River Almond on the west, and from the boundary of the Sheriffdom of Edinburgh on the south to the middle of the Firth of Forth on the north. It was an impressive expansion of influence, to be followed a few years later by the purchase of 17 acres of the lands of High Riggs from the Laird of Inverleith, and in due course the Barony of Portsburgh was formed by royal charter in 1649.

Easter Portsburgh took in the areas of Bristo and Potterrow and the adjoining land bounded on the east by today's Roxburgh Place and on the south by Surgeons' Hall and Nicolson Square. The Wester Portsburgh was the land bounded approximately by the Vennel, the eastern part of King's Stables Road, Main Point, Tollcross and Lauriston, with an extension as far as Bruntsfield Links. In 1856 the old barony, each portion ruled over by a town baillie, was merged into Edinburgh.

In their day, Easter and Wester Portsburgh attracted men of influence and wealth with the mansion houses of people such as the Earl of Wemyss, Hog of Newliston, Borthwick of Crookston and the Earl of Leven situated there. Easter Portsburgh is also said to have boasted 'a great square court ... with buildings and brave houses about it to the very wall of the city'. Other notable residents included the Baron of Inverleith and in the 17th and 18th centuries the Marquis of Douglas and Sir James Nicolson, remembered in Nicolson Street and Square.

While houses continued in the main to be fairly plain on the exterior, two major buildings which continue to grace the town have their origins in the 17th century. Both have been altered, one through the 'improvement' drive of the 19th century and the other through neccessity following damage by fire.

PARLIAMENT HOUSE

Parliament House came about after pressure from Charles I. He was concerned that the New Tolbooth was inadequate as a meeting place for the Council, the Lords of Session and Parliament, and an overflow into St Giles' Kirk was being met with some opposition from those who wanted to return that building fully to a house of worship. Charles seems to have made it very clear to the Town Council that he wanted suitable accommodation, and Sir James Murray of Kilbaberton, His Majesty's Master of Works, was appointed to supervise the job.

The chosen site was on a slope between St Giles' and the Cowgate. It was not until 1640 that Parliament House was completed at a cost of nearly £127,000 Scots, some of that raised by public subscription and the remaining two-thirds by municipal loans.

Parliament House in its original form was completed in 1640 and was used by the Scottish Parliament as a meeting place until the Treaty of Union in 1707 created a British Parliament in London. The attractive frontage was dramatically altered with the construction of the classical façade by Robert Reid in the early 19th century, linked with an expansion of the court buildings and the formation of the Signet and Advocates' Libraries.

Two large halls were formed in the building – Parliament Hall itself, with its great oak-beamed roof and the Laigh Hall below, resting on the top of the undercroft needed to support construction on a steep slope. It has been suggested that if Parliament House had been built on a more manageable site at the foot of the slope and with a Cowgate frontage, the whole city might have developed on different lines, the Cowgate in particular benefiting.

The original shape of Parliament House can only be seen from old drawings, which show rectangular turrets and the principal entrance in the eastern wall of the main building between the figures of Justice and Mercy. The figures were later taken into the building. Many other changes, internal and external, have taken place.

Lord Cockburn, the Scottish judge who wrote so many vivid descriptions of life in old Edinburgh, was one of the to whom those changes were anathema.

'When I first knew it, Parliament House both outside and in, was a curious and interesting place,' he recalls in *Memorials of his Times*.

No one who remembers the old exterior can see the new one without sorrow and indignation. Parliament Square (as foppery now calls it,

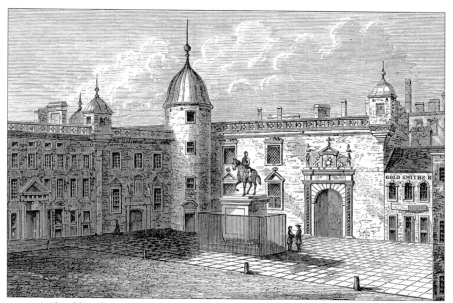

The old Parliament Close became known as Parliament Square, and one of those who protested vigorously about the covering up of the old frontage of Parliament House was Lord Cockburn, the judge and enthusiastic Edinburgh-lover. He deplored what he thought was the 'profanation' of covering up the old building.

but which used, and ought, to be called Parliament *Close)* was then, as now, enclosed on the north by St Giles' Cathedral, on the west by the Outer House, and on the south, partly by courts and partly by shops, above which were very tall houses, and on the east by a line of shops and houses of the same grand height. So that the courts formed the south-west angle of the Close. The old building exhibited some respectable turrets, some ornamental windows and doors, and a handsome balustrade. But the charm that ought to have saved it, was its colour and age, which, however, were the very things that caused its destruction. About 170 years had breathed over it a grave grey hue. The whole aspect was venerable and appropriate; becoming the air and character of a sanctuary of Justice. But a mason pronounced it to be all *'Dead Wall'.*

The officials to whom, at a period when there was no public taste in Edinburgh, this was addressed, believed him; and the two fronts were removed in order to make way for the bright freestone and contemptible decorations that now disgrace us. The model having been laid down, has been copied on all subsequent occasions; till at last the old Parliament Close would not be known by the lawyers or senators who walked through it in the days of the Stuarts, or of the first two of the Guelphs. I cannot doubt that King Charles tried to spur his horse against the Vandals when he saw the profanation begin. But there was such an utter absence of public spirit in Edinburgh then, that the building might have been painted scarlet without anyone objecting.

TRON KIRK

The Tron Kirk was the other building to adorn the High Street, again a suggestion for a new church coming from Charles I, who had raised St Giles' to a bishopric and wanted to remove from it the partitions which divided it for use by four separate congregations. In fact, he wanted two new churches, but the Town Council appeared to struggle to meet the expense of the Tron Kirk – planned in 1635 and not ready till 1645, with further work still to be done.

In 1637 the site in the High Street was secured – the second church which was to have been placed on Castlehill was never built – and John Mylne, Master Mason to the Crown and the town, was placed in charge. It was not finished until 26 years later, although it was in use long before completion, the first seat rents being taken in 1647.

The inscription carved above the door describes the building as Christ's Church, although it was called the Tron Kirk because of the weigh tron, or public weighing beam, nearby in the High Street. This was often described as the Salt Tron, to distinguish it from the Butter Tron in the Weigh-house further up the street.

The church was tight up against High Street tenements until the construction of South Bridge and Hunter Square in the 1780s, when the old buildings were demolished for the new streets. The church was shortened at that time in its east, west and south sides. It continued as a place of worship into the 1960s, although another major alteration was enforced in the 19th century. Its Dutch steeple was destroyed in the Great Fire of 1824, when the church itself was under threat from the flames.

A worshipper in the church was heard praying one Sunday: 'God bless all fools and idiots, and particularly the Magistrates of Edinburgh.' The steeple bell – poet Robert Fergusson's 'crazy, dinsome thing' – melted in the 1824 fire, after which the present steeple was built.

In its secular form, it has resisted suggestions over the years that it might

The Dutch steeple of the Tron Kirk was a familiar sight for Edinburgh folk, but it fell to the Great Fire of 1824, when the church itself narrowly escaped serious damage. No one could believe that the old church would be affected by fire, and one old woman declared that the calamity of the Great Fire generally was a sign of God's wrath over the music festival held in the city shortly before .

be demolished to make an easier traffic flow in the High Street and the Bridges. There was a proposal at one time that its great spire should be removed and replaced with one in the original Dutch style, but that was put aside. In recent tines it has been a Tourist Information Centre for the Old Town and is likely to become a restaurant complex.

When the floor of the interior was lifted during restoration work some years after the congregation left in 1952, the remains of part of Marlyn's Wynd, which ran down to the Cowgate, were found and they provide an interesting feature of Edinburgh lost and found.

While the church, sited between houses in the High Street, did not involve any major alterations to the plan of the old town, apart from the demolition to clear the site, the building of Parliament House was another story.

> The site was that of the ministers' houses, formerly the dwellings of the Provost and prebendaries of the collegiate foundation of St Giles' with the abandoned burial yards lying between them and the church and also to the south down to the Cowgate [Dr Marguerite Wood, the former Keeper of the City Records, has explained].

> The Parliament House and its close, now known as Parliament Square, became a focus for much of the life of the burgh and some

years later the unbuilt ground to the east became the site of an early venture in planned building. The Council after the Restoration made an attempt to turn part of the ground to the south and east of the Parliament House into a garden for the ardornment of the town. The plan failed, partly, it seems, because of their almost inevitable habit of imposing so many restrictions that the venture could not pay, partly in all probability because the ground was too valuable as a building site.

But again the High Street was to be hit by a series of fires which would destroy old property and cause rebuilding. In 1674 several tenements in the south-east section of the street around South Gray's Close were lost, and the Council ordered that wood should not be used in their rebuilding. They also instructed that 'pillars and arches' be formed at street level.

Two years later, another huge fire destroyed the block to the east of St Giles' and Parliament Close and at the top of the Kirkheugh, the wynd running to the Cowgate. The Privy Council saw a chance and ordered that the entry to Parliament Close should be widened from a mere pedestrian passageway to 30 feet to allow carriage access.

The rebuilding of the fire site was tackled in the main by Thomas Robertson, a merchant, and the scheme included a new meal market in stone, houses to the north of the market and on the east side of the Kirkheugh, on part of the waste land behind Parliament House, and on the east side of Parliament Close. The plan also included an Exchange building for the town's merchants and more houses on the south side of Parliament Close.

One mighty tenement hereabouts is said to have been 15 storeys high from the Cowgate view. Robertson's Exchange appears to have fallen foul of both the Town and Privy Councils, who constantly interfered with their own suggestions for alterations to his plans.

'Unfortunately, because of the short life of the building no plan or illustration of it exists,' says Dr Wood.

The descriptions of it in the Council minutes are not precise and it is difficult to picture it. That arches formed part of the front is known by the facts that the Privy Council wished them built up.

That carving was used is stated in a Town Council minute which suggests that, as costly additions to the original plan had been made, Robertson should receive a supplementary payment from the Privy Council. There must have been a hall where the merchants could meet, but this is never mentioned. All that appears from the descrip-

tions is that a black and white marble paved passage ran through the
building lined with booths or shops, some of which were sold to the
Edinburgh merchants, while apparently Robertson retained others in
his own hands for letting, doubtless to recoup himself for his expenses.

Above this, the street level, were chambers bought by Government officials and houses or flats. The description, however, does not
mention to how many storeys the building rose.

The Exchange building was finished about 1683, but whoever used it did so for
only a short time. Fire again, on a disastrous scale, destroyed the Exchange and
many of the other tenements in Parliament Close in 1700. The blaze started in
the north-east corner of the Meal Market in the Cowgate, within a small court
of buildings, mostly occupied by lawyers, directly behind the Parliament Close.
It was late evening in February, and the fire spread rapidly up the hill,
destroyed the Kirkheugh buildings and raged into the High Street. The 15-
storey-high tenements, the highest in the town, were engulfed.

A dramatic description of the fire was given in a letter by Duncan Forbes
to his brother:

Dear Brother,
My last was with humbling news, and this with news more humbling.
Upon Saturday night, by ten o'clock, a fire broke out in Mr. John
Buchan's closet-window, towards the Meal Market. It continued till
eleven o'clock of the day with the greatest fervour and vehemency
that ever I saw fire do, notwithstanding that I saw London burn.

'There are burnt, by the easiest computation, between three and
four hundred families; all the pride of Edinburgh is sunk; from the
Cowgate to the High Street all is burnt, and hardly one stone is left
upon another. The Commissioner, the President of Parliament, the
President of the Court of Session, the Bank, most of the Lords,
lawyers, and clerks, were all burnt, besides many poor and great
families. It is said just now by Sir John Cochran and Jordanhill that
there is more rent burnt in this fire than the whole city of Glasgow
will amount to. The Parliament House very nearly escaped; all
registers confounded; Clerks' Chambers and processes in such a
confusion that the Lords and Officers of State are just now met in
Ross's Tavern, in order to adjourn the Session by means of the
disorder. Few people are lost, if any at all: but there was neither heart
nor hand left among them for saving from the fire, nor a drop of water

in the cisterns. Twenty thousand hands flitting their trash, they know not where, and hardly twenty at work. These Babels, of ten and fourteen storey high, are down to the ground, and their fall is very terrible. Many rueful spectacles, such as Corserig (a judge) naked, with a child under his oxter, hopping for his life. The Fish Market, and all from the Cowgate to Pett Street's Close burnt; The Exchange, vaults, and coal cellars under the Parliament Close, are still burning. This epitome of dissolution, I send to you, without saying any more, but that the Lord is angry with us and I see no intercessor.

Your loving brother to serve you,

D Forbes.

The Parliament Close was rebuilt in a uniform style of architecture 'and, till the erection of the New Town, was by far the most splendid piece of building in the city', says Robert Chambers, the antiquarian writer and historian.

The height of the largest tenements in the rebuilding was also lowered to 11 storeys, exclusive of garrets. Another great fire a century later would ironically seal their fate and provide the opportunity for a new-look Parliament Square, which exists today.

Two little footnotes to the 17th-century Edinburgh are gleaned from the Burgh records.

On 8 September 1697, Sir James Stewart, his Majesty's Advocate, was granted permission to straighten the foot of the close where he lived (Advocate's Close) to the width of four feet with a view to enclosing the waste ground there which was being used as a common 'jaques'.

On May 4 the following year, the Council 'disponed to Samuel McLellan, present Town Treasurer, ruinous houses, waste ground and yard, sometime belonging to the heirs and representatives of the deceased Robert Davidson, merchant in Edinburgh, lying in the Castlehill; also the waste yard adjacent thereto'.

Adjustments, minor and major, were always being made in the closes. Old houses were hauled down and new ones built.

OPPOSITE.

Advocate's Close runs from the High Street northwards down the slope to what was the bank of the Nor' Loch. Named after Sir James Stewart, Lord Advocate between 1692 and 1709 and from 1711 to 1713, the close still has some of the oldest houses in the city in its upper reaches, but in the late 19th century most of the buildings lower down were swept away. Nevertheless, it is still one of the most evocative of the old closes.

CHAPTER 5
COMETH THE MAN

The time of great change, or at least the start of great change for Edinburgh came early in the 18th century. The town was slipping into a state of decay and despair, not helped by the previous fires which many believed were a punishment from God. The ill-fated scheme to found a Scottish trading colony on the isthmus of Darien had seen many losing their investment, and some had also lost husbands and sons to the expeditions. Ships foundered at sea and disease ravaged those who made it to the promised land, only to be attacked by Spanish troops.

It was a disaster of monumental proportions for Scotland, and when news of the Darien failure reached the town in 1700, mobs took to the streets in a fury of retribution for the collapse of the company which had been set up to trade with Africa and the Indies. Strong feelings were also expressed against King William in London, who was seen to have supported the English East India Company and not given any backing to the Scottish enterprise.

Within a few years, further concern was expressed about moves to unite the Scottish Parliament with that of England, and the Treaty of Union in 1707 was far from generally acclaimed. For Edinburgh, it was seen as yet another move to diminish its importance and influence. There was a simmering unrest which in many ways finally erupted in the 1736 Porteous Riot already mentioned. One report on the immediate effect of the Union, quoted in the *Book of the Old Edinburgh Club*, summed up bleakly:

> In the towns the grass grew round the market crosses; the east coast trade was destroyed, and the west was undeveloped; the arsenals were emptied, the fortresses disarmed, and two Royal palaces fell into ruin.

Edinburgh was in the doldrums, an air of lethargy hung over the population, probably around 25,000 in 1700. Old houses were decaying, and some simply collapsed; the streets and closes were dirty and in need of repair. The first half of the century has been described as the Dark Age of Edinburgh.

MERCHANT MAIDEN HOSPITAL

There were a few bright spots in the general gloom, such as the foundation of the Merchant Maiden Hospital. The Company of Merchants of Edinburgh, founded in 1681, were approached by a wealthy widow, Mrs Mary Hair, whose

The Merchant Maiden Hospital was founded through the generosity of a wealthy widow, Mrs Mary Hair. It opened in the Merchants' Hall in the Cowgate before moving to a house in its own grounds at Bristo and then to Archibald Place. Originally providing accommodation for 'poor children of the female sex', it was one of the hospital schools which followed the pattern set by George Heriot. The Merchant Maiden Hospital is now the Mary Erskine School.

maiden name was Erskine. Her proposal was to provide a charitable foundation, or hospital school as it was known in those days, 'for maintaining and educating poor children of the female sex'.

This would follow the example of the magnificent George Heriot's Hospital, which was started in 1620 but not fully completed till around the end of the century. Heriot, 'Jinglin' Geordie', treasurer to James VI and I, had left his fortune to provide education and accommodation for 'faitherless bairns' and the day school, as it is now, is still one of the finest buildings in the city.

The girls' school was finally opened in the Merchants' Hall in the Cowgate, probably taking its first pupils in 1696, as the Merchant Maiden Hospital. Within a decade, it had outgrown the premises, and in 1706 Mrs Hair provided more money to buy a house 'with large and pleasant gardens' just outside the town wall and close to the Bristo Port, 'towards the use of a hospital to be called the Hospital of Mary Erskine'.

In 1818 the expanding hospital moved to a new Grecian-style building in the gently rising ground of what was to become Archibald Place, off Lauriston Place and to the west of Lauriston Lane on the edge of the Meadows. The building was later used by George Watson's Boys' College.

In 1870 the various hospital schools administered by the Merchant Company were converted to day schools. The Merchant Maiden Hospital became the Edinburgh Institution for Young Ladies, moving to Queen Street in the New Town. Eventually the Mary Erskine School for Girls, as it was renamed, moved in 1966 to its present location on the old Ravelston Estate on the west of the city, both the grounds and old mansion house being purchased to create a new school and environment. An office block rose on the abandoned Queen Street site.

TRADES MAIDEN HOSPITAL

Mary Erskine also endowed in 1704 the Trades Maiden Hospital, which was built on the west side of Horse Wynd beside Argyle Square. It was to provide shelter and education for the daughters of 'decayed tradesmen' and was promoted by the Trades Incorporations in the town 'excited by the good example of the Company of Merchants'.

Described as a 'plain substantial edifice' with a central block and a great arched door, the Trades Maiden Hospital was demolished to make way for Chambers Street, created under the City Improvement Act of 1867. The hospital moved to Rillbank, near the Meadows.

Mary Erskine also provided money to help to endow the Trades Maiden Hospital at the corner of Argyle Square and Horse Wynd, both demolished to make way for Chambers Street. The hospital building was described as 'having nothing particular in its appearance to attract attention' and provided an upbringing for daughters of members of the Incorporation of Trades who had fallen into 'decayed circumstances'.

Cometh the Hour ...

The man who was to be the driving force and visionary for Edinburgh was George Drummond, who was to serve six terms as Lord Provost, spread over a period of more than 40 years. It was in 1725 that he was first appointed to the post and, says his biographer, William Baird,

> Drummond early realised the necessity for improved house accommodation for the citizens. Crowded and huddled together as they were within the city walls, the sanitary condition was deplorable. There was undoubtedly great picturesqueness in the piles of buildings with their wooden-faced gables and high pitched roofs, but the beauty was terribly marred by filthy streets and closes, whose pavement, rugged and broken, was odorous and slippery, and down whose gutters ran the refuse of a crowded population, among which the pigs stuck their snouts in grunting satisfaction for garbage.
>
> Even the houses of the better class were small, and often so

crowded with furniture that beds were sometimes to be found in handsome drawing-rooms, while servants slept under the dresser in the kitchen, or even in a drawer which was made to shut during the day!

If not commodious enough, they were cheap, for we are seriously told that the common rent of a gentleman's dwelling in a flat, up to the first half of the eighteenth century was £8 or £10 a year. The long steep stairs leading to the different flats were crowded all day long with men, women and children going and coming to their homes; beside the stream of porters carrying coals, Musselburgh fishwives hawking their fish, sweeps, water-carriers and barbers, all jostling unceremoniously as they pressed past each other in the close or stairway.

One compensation for the increasing overcrowdedness as the town continued to rise higher within its limited confines behind the wall and the Nor' Loch was

The foundation stone of the Royal Infirmary was laid in August 1738 following the successful opening of the first small public hospital in Robertson's Close, off the Cowgate. One of the driving forces in both these enterprises was George Drummond, the man who was Lord Provost of Edinburgh on six occasions. The Royal Infirmary was in Infirmary Street until its move to the new building in Lauriston Place in the 1870s and is now at Little France.

the great social mix living within the tenements, with judges rubbing shoulders with beggars. The town, too, was coming to terms with the new style of building layout provided in Milne's Court in the Lawnmarket and Mylne's Square further down the High Street. These were improvements carried out by private enterprise on sites cleared for the purpose at the instigation of the Council which had powers to acquire compulsorily derelict properties. The tenement buildings were constructed around small squares, providing an element of better lighting and ventilation for the flats.

The square of 1689 was demolished in 1899 to clear the site for *The Scotsman* building, completed in 1902, but Milne's Court (1690), minus its original western side, stands much renovated, still with its striking frontage to the Lawnmarket, previously 'arising stark and square built amid the many timber fronted gables and symbolising a new age'.

These projects helped to bring a new thinking into the 18th century and were followed, for example, by James Court, also in the Lawnmarket – again, high tenements around a small square, and providing large flats for prosperous citizens and plenty of other accommodation in the same building for poorer folk. In clearing away the sites for such developments, the old timber-fronted and low-standing houses were swept away and the towering, solid-stone tenements, capable of standing for centuries, as they prove today, came into their own.

Drummond, as a driving influence, was instrumental in achieving the aim of forming a public infirmary – first of all in a small building at the head of Robertson's Close off the Cowgate on land formerly held by the Black Friars' monastery. This led to the creation of the Royal Infirmary in Infirmary Street, which was transferred in 1873 to Lauriston Place. The first small infirmary building was cleared in 1785, when South Bridge was built.

Drummond saw that the Old Town had to expand if it was to survive. The population was increasing rapidly, doubling to about 50,000 by the middle of the century.

His eyes were on the open country to the north, on the other side of the increasingly stagnant water which had outlived its use as an obstacle to invasion and was more the dumping ground for the town's household debris.

By his third term as Lord Provost in 1750, there was a growing feeling in the town that something positive had to be done. More tenements were becoming dilapidated and dangerous, the sanitation problems were worsening and the more prosperous who could afford a mansion house in the country were moving out. On the extremities of the town itself were signs of new thinking. Argyle Square, 'late begun' in 1745, offered terraced houses round a garden area and proved an attractive proposition, as did Alison Square, which was built a few years later in the form of an H-shaped tenement.

But the major move came in 1752 with the publication of *Proposals for carrying on certain Public Works in the City of Edinburgh*. The pamphlet was published under the name of Sir George Elliott, but there is little doubt that Drummond had a major input. The Convention of Royal Burghs in July of that year had resolved to build an exchange for the city's merchants, a place to store Scotland's records, a building where the Council could meet, as well as other improvements in the city. The 7,500-word pamphlet was authorised by the Convention 'explaining and recommending' their design.

The timing for such a development was highly appropriate. The pamphlet set out in its preamble:

> The narrow limits of the royalty of Edinburgh and the want of certain public buildings and other useful and ornamental accommodations in the city, having been long regretted, an opportunity of remedying these inconviences was often wished for, and Providence has now furnished a very fair one. In September last the side wall of a building of six storeys high, in which several families lived, gave way all of a sudden ... This melancholy accident occasioned a general survey to be made of the old houses; and such as were insufficient were pulled down; so that several of the principal parts of the town were laid in ruins.

The proposals, in short, were:

To build an exchange upon the ruins on the north side of the High Street.

To erect upon the ruins in Parliament Square a building for law courts and the Town Council, 'several registers,' and the advocates' library.

To obtain an Act of Parliament to extend the royalty.

To enlarge and beautify the town by opening new streets to the north and south, removing the markets and shambles, and turning the Nor' Loch into a canal with walks and terraces on both sides.

Drummond, no longer Provost, but in his role as Grand Master of the Grand Lodge of Scotland, laid the foundation stone of the Royal Exchange on 3 September 1753 – the building which is now the heart of the City Chambers. The site was bounded on the east 'by the west gable stone land commonly called Fairholm's Land, and bounded on the west by the entry to the tenement called Writers Court, the stone land immediately below Allan's Close, the High Street on the south and the Lake commonly called the Nor' Loch on the north part, being 150 feet from east to west on the south boundary'.

Incorporated into the Exchange were shops and houses and a Customs House, but the merchants subsequently resisted a move there, preferring to do their business around the Mercat Cross or in the coffee houses, their traditional meeting places.

MERCAT CROSS

Whether as an act against those dissenting merchants or as a genuine attempt to free up the High Street to the ever-increasing traffic, a decision was taken in 1756 to remove the Mercat Cross, which had been rebuilt and resited in 1617. There is record of the cross as far back as 1365 showing that it stood at that time on the south side of the High Street about 45 feet east of the present east end of St Giles'. In 1617, to widen the thoroughfare for the visit of James VI and I it was taken down and recreated further down the High Street.

Hugo Arnot says: 'The building was an octagon of 16 feet diameter, and about 15 feet high; besides the pillar in the centre, at each angle there was an Ionick pillar, from the top of which a species of Gothick bastion projected; and between the columns there were modern arches.'

The structure was decorated with medallions which featured carved heads and also sported the town crest. The cross was a focal point. From its platform proclamations were made, and crowds gathered for celebrations. It was also a place of punishment and occasional execution, particularly of the high and mighty who had been found guilty of treason.

The column rising from the platform was upwards of 20 feet high and 18 inches in diameter, and according to Arnot, 'spangled with thistles and adorned with a Corinthian capital, upon the top of which was an unicorn'.

But in 1756, despite its long history and association with the town, it was to go. In its removal the pillar was broken, and taken to Drum House at Gilmerton, where it remained until 1885. That year, William Ewart Gladstone, Prime Minister and MP for Midlothian, paid for a complete restoration of the Mercat Cross, which was placed in the centre of the roadway at the east end of St Giles' – only a short distance away from the site it had occupied in the 14th century.

The present shaft was placed in 1970 and is a replica of the fragments rebuilt in 1885. It is several feet shorter than the medieval one.

The place where the 1756 cross stood is marked by an octagon of cobbles on the High Street, close to the entrance to Old Fishmarket Close. Five of the medallions mentioned above eventually found their way to Sir Walter Scott, who had them built into the garden wall of his Borders home at Abbotsford.

The poet Claudero again gave vent to his feelings with 'The last Speech and dying Words of the Cross of Edinburgh, which was hanged, drawn and quartered on Monday the 15th March 1756, for the Horrid Crime of being an Incumbrance to the Street'.

> Ye sons of Scotia, mourn and weep,
> Express your grief with sorrow deep

are the opening lines of his poem, in which he suggests that the Cross was demolished because its antique and somewhat tattered appearance shamed the handsome frontage of the new Exchange.

CHAPTER 6

'LONG BLACK SNAIL'

With the wind of change now flowing through the High Street at least, the next stage in progressing the proposals saw another swatch of old houses go for the construction of a bridge from the town's ridge across the valley of the Nor' Loch to provide an access to the open land where a residential suburb could be built.

Drummond again laid the foundation stone for what was a complicated engineering operation to throw a bridge 'over the east end of the North Loch, at least 40 feet between the parapets of the said bridge, and upon an equal declivity of one foot in 16 from the High Street at the Cap and Feather Close in a straight line to the opposite side leading to Multrees-hill,' as the advertisement calling for tenders put it.

In October 1763, in his role as Acting Grand Master, Drummond performed the ceremony, but it was almost two years before the contract was signed, with a completion date scheduled for November 1769, by which time Drummond was in his grave. Early in 1769, the bridge was open for pedestrians, but in August part of the sidewalls of an abutment collapsed, killing five people. The three-arched bridge was completed in 1772, although alterations continued to be made for some years.

The original bridge, designed by William Mylne, was widened by 7 feet in 1873, and between 1894 and 1897 it was replaced by a steel bridge, the design of which, by Cunningham, Blyth and Westland, was fitted to the expanding Waverley Station below.

The North Bridge created the first major gap in the run of buildings on the north side of the High Street, after the Exchange, and brought to an end the life of such closes as the Cap and Feather, where the poet Robert Fergusson was born.

Fergusson was described by his fellow poet Robert Burns as 'my elder brother in misfortune, by far my elder brother in the muses' and died a young man in the Bedlam at Bristo, the result of his dissolute living and a fall in 1774.

The Nor' Loch lay in the valley of what is now Princes Street Gardens and provided a defensive obstacle on that side of the town from the 15th century. The start of the construction of the first North Bridge in 1763 saw a partial draining of the water, and by 1764 the Town Council recorded it was 'now in good measure drained'. In 1787 the Council ordered the complete drainage of the loch's site 'with all possible dispatch'.

Burns paid to have a stone raised on Fergusson's unmarked grave in the Canongate Kirkyard. It still stands today, not far from the splendid new statue of Fergusson on the pavement outside the church gate.

With an access to the north and the development of what came to be known as the New Town in the area bounded now by Princes and Queen Streets and St Andrew and Charlotte Squares, it was only to be expected that the city would spread southwards as well. Indeed that was envisaged in the proposals.

Already there were Argyle and Alison Squares. Brown Square followed in 1765, a development projected by the builder James Brown and described as 'an extremely elegant improvement'. Its last remnants were lost in the 1960s, when the site was cleared in preparation for the extension to the Royal Scottish Museum in Chambers Street. Earlier improvements, including the creation of George IV Bridge and Chambers Street, had sliced through other sides of the scheme of townhouses.

Brown went on to build George Square. It was started in 1766, a year before the first New Town house foundation stone was laid by James Craig in what is now Thistle Court, behind George Street. George's Square, as it was originally called, was named after Brown's brother and was one of the finest addresses in Edinburgh until the heart was ripped out of it in the 20th century.

What was seen as being needed for southward expansion was another bridge spanning the Cowgate and heading past the university buildings on the former Kirk o' Field grounds. In May 1785, the South Bridge Act was approved in Parliament. There was some dispute about a starting point for the bridge from the High Street, but the level of the street was finally lowered by five or 6 feet at the Tron Kirk and the foundation stone was laid on 1 August 1785.

Properties lost as the bridge was constructed and Blair Street down to the Cowgate formed were in Niddry's, Marlyn's and Peebles Wynds. With the destruction of part of Niddry's Wynd in particular went some of the most 'interesting fabrics of an early date', says Wilson.

One of the grandest houses in the narrow alley, and indeed in the town itself, was the civic palace, as it was described, of Nicol Uddert or Edward, Provost, in 1592. It was a large, quadrangular building which provided a grand residence fit for King James VI and his queen for a while during Edward's provostship. Always short of money, it was the king's wont to descend on prosperous citizens for his board and lodgings and expect to be well treated.

The house stood halfway down the west side of the wynd, and was later called Lockhart Court, being the town house of the Lockharts of Carnwath. On the opposite side of the wynd was the house occupied by the family of Erskine of Mar.

Robert Chambers recounts that in another house to the north of the Mar residence was a shop kept by an 'eccentric personage' who exhibited a sign with the inscription 'Orra Things Bought and Sold'.

> ... which signified he dealt in odd articles, such as a single shoe-buckle, one of a pair of skates, a tea-pot wanting a lid, or perhaps, as often, a lid *minus* a tea-pot; in short, any unpaired article which is not to be got in the shops where only new things were sold, and which, nevertheless, are now and then as indispensably wanted by house-holders as anything else.

Some of the houses had a double entry from Niddry's and Marlyn's Wynd (where earlier houses were removed for the building of the new church).

The author Henry Mackenzie, who died in 1832, pointed out one of the problems this sometimes created:

I remember a mistake of a lady's chair man in carrying her, first to a wrong door in the one wynd, when she was ushered into a drawing room, where, when she discovered her mistake, she made her apology and returned to her chair, the bearers of which were directed to go to the house she wished to go to, of which the proper door was in the other wynd.

She was carried there accordingly, but unluckily to the other entry of the very house she had left, and on being admitted she was ushered into the self-same drawing room.

BLACK TURNPIKE

Also lost was the formidable Black Turnpike, which stood on the site of the present corner of the High Street and Hunter Square. With three turnpike stairs, it was then the second house west of the Tron Kirk and adjoined Clam Shell land – you can still see a clam shell on the High Street frontage – and was traditionally the house of Sir Simon Preston, the Provost, where Queen Mary was brought by her captors in 1567 after her surrender at Carberry Hill and before her year's incarceration in Loch Leven Castle.

Wilson describes the ancient Black Turnpike as 'one of the most sumptious edifices of the old town.' There was a popular belief in its fabulous antiquity, some going so far as to assert it was built by King Kenneth, the last of that name being killed in 1005. Whatever its origins, there is no doubt it was a fine old building. 'The edifice commonly called the Black Turnpike, immediately to the west of the Tron Church, at the head of Peebles Wynd, one of the oldest stone buildings upon record in Edinburgh is now begun to be pulled down ...' was how the *Caledonian Mercury* newspaper of 15 May 1788, recorded its demise.

GUARD HOUSE

In front of the Turnpike in the centre of the street stood the bleak guard house. 'If the cross was removed as a nuisance,' observes Arnot, 'a much greater one is allowed to remain, the town guard house, a huge misshapen bulk.'

Sir Walter Scott memorably described it as a 'long black snail crawling up the middle of the High Street and deforming its beautiful esplanade'.

Across the road from Bell's Wynd, the New Assembly Close and Stevenlaw's Close, the guardhouse was built probably at the close of the 17th or

One of the finest buildings in the High Street was known as the Black Turnpike, to which some attributed an almost legendary antiquity. It was occupied by George Crighton, Bishop of Dunkeld, in the 16th century and it was certainly regarded as a very old dwelling when it was demolished in 1788. The guard house stood out in the High Street in front of the Black Turnpike and was almost universally regarded as one of the least attractive buildings in the town. Many wondered how it survived as long as 1785, but it housed the City Guard, the band of men who were finally replaced after the formation of a regular police force in 1805. Beside the house was a wooden horse on which guardsmen had to sit as a punishment for minor offences. Once the building went, traffic flow in the High Street was much smoother.

beginning of the 18th century for the City Guard, a forerunner to the present-day police force. It was a one-storey building with four apartments. On the west and south-west corner was the Captain's room, adjoining on the north the Burghers' room, a place for prisoners. In the centre was the common hall and on the east the accommodation for the city chimney sweeps, who were called the Tron men. Under the floor was a vaulted hall, called the black hole, where rowdy prisoners were placed. In all, it was 70 feet long by 40 feet wide.

Its removal, says Wilson, was prolonged as it was 'protected by its

ungainly utility from the destruction which befell many a building of rare historical interest'. In 1785, however, doom was pronounced and the guardsmen moved into New Assembly Close until the guard was disbanded in 1817 – 'Their final refuge was demolished, the last of them were put on the town's pension list, and the truncheon of the constable replaced the venerable firelock and the Lochaber-axe.'

The extension of the town north and southwards saw a gradual, yet steady, exodus of families to the new houses which were gracing new streets. The old properties in the Lawnmarket and High Street were then facing further dereliction as they passed into the hands of landlords anxious to obtain rents without any great expenditure on upkeep.

In the *Statistical Account of Scotland*, edited by Sir John Sinclair and finally completed in 1799, we get a fair idea of many of the changes which occured fairly quickly in Edinburgh in the latter years of the century. The publisher William Creech, who became Lord Provost in 1811, made comparisons for the Account:

> In 1763 – people of quality and fashion lived in houses which, in 1783, were inhabited by tradesmen, or by people in humble and ordinary life. The Lord Chief Justice Clerk Tinwald's house was possessed by a French teacher – Lord President Craigie's house, by a rouping-wife or saleswoman of old furniture – and Lord Drunmore's house was left by a chairman for want of accommodation.

He adds that the house of the Duke of Douglas at the (time of) Union, was now possessed by a wheel-wright. 'Oliver Cromwell once lived in the late gloomy chambers of the Sheriff Clerk. The great Marquis of Argyle's house, in the Castlehill, was possessed by a hosier, at £12 per annum.'

The year 1789, reports Creech, saw the laying of the foundation stone for 'a magnificant New College – the old college having become ruinous, and the classrooms unfit to contain the number of students who resorted to this celebrated school of science and literature'.

OPPOSITE.
Pushing ever upwards as the town grew in population, the houses in the Lawnmarket followed the traditional style of an outside stair for access to the higher flats with shops or business premises on street level.

The Royal High School has its origins in an Act of Council of 1519, when it was decreed no bairns should be put to any school in Edinburgh 'bot to the principal Grammar Scule of the samyn'. After renting a property in the Cowgate, the Council agreed in 1578 to build a school in what became the High School Yards. A later building started in 1777 still stands as part of the University of Edinburgh properties at the foot of Infirmary Street, although the school moved to Regent Road into the Thomas Hamilton-designed Greek Revival building (1825–29). The school is now at Barnton.

HIGH SCHOOL

A 'new, elegant and commodious edifice' for a grammar school was built in 1777 (in High School Yards), and that meant the old schoolhouse built in the garden of the former monastery of the Black Friars was no more.

The town's grammar school, now the Royal High School, was originally attached to Holyrood Abbey. It came under the control of the magistrates of Edinburgh early in the 16th century, when it was in a building on the southern slopes of the Cowgate valley. The school seems to have been rebuilt in 1554 when a house at the foot of Blackfriars' Wynd was rented to provide temporary accommodation for the boy scholars.

In 1578 the school was moved to a purpose-built schoolhouse in the monastery grounds, but two centuries later it needed to be expanded to cope with the increasing pupil numbers. This resulted in the construction of the 1777 building, which was placed on an adjoining site where it still stands, at the foot of Infirmary Street beside the old Royal Infirmary block and the former surgical hospital. It is now part of the university complex there.

The spectacular Royal High School in Regent Road, one of the finest buildings in the New Town, was formed between 1825 and 1829 and served as an educational establishment until the 1960s, when the school moved to Barnton.

THE NOR' LOCH

Another major feature to disappear was the Nor' Loch. For centuries it had provided a reassurance to the citizens that the town had a northern defence. It was created around the time of the 1450 wall, when the Council had considered building a fosse or moat in the glacial valley below the Castle. There was an abundant source of water from springs beneath the rock, and it was decided to form a permanent loch with a dam and sluice gates at the eastern end.

The loch stretched from the former garden of King David, close to St Cuthbert's Church, down to the line of Halkerston's Wynd, where the North Bridge came to be built.

For three centuries the loch was used as a dumping ground for rubbish of all sorts, including the entrails of slaughtered animals, and as a place of punishment. People were drowned there as a form of execution, those accused of witchcraft might be put to the test of water, and the town's 'dooking stool' was used for minor offences.

The witchcraft persecutions of the 16th and 17th centuries saw many an accused woman thrown into the loch with her hands and feet bound. If she floated, that was proof of guilt. If she sank and drowned she was innocent of witchcraft. Not much consolation for the victim, but such was justice in Edinburgh those stormy days. The more common punishment for those convicted of witchcraft (often a confession came after torture by thumbscrews or even the boot – planks of wood strapped round the leg with wedges driven in to crush the limb in excrutiating pain) was to be 'worryt' (strangled) at the stake at the Castlehill and burned while still at least partially alive.

On the edge of the Castle Esplanade there is the witches' fountain, a little memorial to those who died in such a terrible way, and a reminder of times most citizens were glad to put behind them. The Witchcraft Act was repealed in 1736.

Once the Nor' Loch was finally drained, the valley became a prime piece of land which many developers eyed greedily. The North Bridge at the eastern end of the valley provided the access from the Old to the New Town and encouraged residents to think about having a house on the developing streets to the north of the loch.

The level of the water in the loch seemed to vary, possibly about 8 feet deep in its wider expanses, though latterly part of it became little more than a marsh. The depth could be controlled by the sluice gates, and for many years there was one particularly deep pool known as the Pot, a favoured spot for suicides. The loch was partially drained at one stage in 1663, while various schemes were proposed to bring the Water of Leith through the valley to freshen up the often stagnant water in the loch.

The construction of North Bridge effectively brought an end to the loch because of the need to construct its piers on dry land. By 1764 the Town Council recorded that the loch was 'now in good measure drained'.

When the Mound came to be formed, initially by dumping cartloads of earth from the excavations for the foundations of the New Town houses, the valley was split in two and the waterflow from the west was cut off. The Council then ordered in 1787 that it should be drained completely 'with all possible dispatch'.

Below the North Bridge, the vegetable market was formed, and a slaughterhouse was sited beside the 'Little Mound' which was created near the present Waverley Bridge. In time, the valley was laid out as ornamental gardens and, of course, the railway companies were allowed to intrude and develop the Waverley Station. Originally, the station terminus for the Edinburgh–Glasgow train was at Haymarket.

In the plan prepared by James Craig for the New Town, a canal is shown, designed as a decorative feature below Princes Street. It never came to pass, although there was a Canal Street.

BURGH LOCH

The Burgh or South Loch covered the ground we know as the Meadows, lying on the edge of the old Burgh Muir. Water was pumped from it by a windmill to supply the brewers of the Society, a company formed under James VI in 1598. From the windmill (Windmill Street off George Square is a reminder of the operation), the water was piped to the Society premises (at the western end of the present Chambers Street) for the brewing of fine ale. The water was certainly purer than that in the polluted Nor' Loch.

In the 17th century the first drainage of the Burgh Loch took place, and for a time it was know as Straiton's Loch, after John Straiton who leased it. It was then let in 1722 to Thomas Hope, who committed himself to draining it and making walkways round the ground. Later it became a public park, and the flat green expanse, protected by Act of Parliament, has resisted various attempts for its development, including a plan to form a racecourse on it.

WRYCHTIS-HOUSIS

Not far from the Burgh Loch was the 'picturesque half-castellated edifice' of Wrychtis-housis, a Napier family mansion house with recorded origins as far back as 1390. Wilson describes it as 'by far the most striking example of an ancient baronial mansion that existed in the neighbourhood of Edinburgh ... the picturesque blending of the rude feudal stronghold with the ornate additions of more peaceful times.' It was in the area of the present Gillespie Crescent, and fell in what one commentator described as an act of vandalism, to the demolishers' hammer in 1800 to make way for James Gillespie's Hospital.

JAMES GILLESPIE'S HOSPITAL

Originally overlooking the west end of Bruntsfield Links, this hospital – 'a tasteless structure' was one description – with its associated school was another of the benefactions of a generous Edinburgh citizen. James Gillespie

Standing on the edge of Bruntsfield Links, James Gillespie's Hospital (and its associated school)
was another example of a prosperous merchant's legacy to the town. Gillespie was a snuff and
tobacco dealer with a shop in the High Street and a mill at Spylaw, Colinton. His hospital
sheltered 'aged persons' and the school educated 100 boys when the building opened in 1802.

made his fortune as a tobacco and snuff merchant operating from a little shop in the High Street – there is a fine plaque marking the spot. His mill was at Spylaw, on the banks of the Water of Leith at Colinton.

Gillespie died in 1797 and left most of his money for the foundation of a hospital for 'aged persons' and a school for 100 boys. 'Aged' was defined as over 55, and residents had to be of good character 'being poor and having no assistance from other charities'. The boys also had to be poor, between the ages of six and twelve, and their basic education was writing and arithmetic, with attention paid 'to the morals and religious principles'.

The demolition of Wrychtis-housis provided the site for the new hospital, designed by William Burn, which opened in 1802 with a school building in its grounds. The institution was managed by the Merchant Company until 1908, when the school passed to the Town Council and moved into the former Boroughmuir school building at the corner of Warrender Park Crescent and Whitehouse Loan in 1914. As James Gillespie's High School for Girls, the building was the inspiration for the Marcia Blane Academy immortalised in Gillespie old girl Muriel Spark's novel, *The Prime of Miss Jean Brodie*.

The hospital building was sold in the 1920s to the Royal Blind Asylum and replaced by a new sheltered housing complex in 1976.

The old village of Wright's Houses gradually disappeared as road widening between Tollcross and Bruntsfield took place. As the development of this area progressed, mansions such as that owned by the Hogs of Newliston (on the corner of today's Lauriston Place and Lauriston Park), the Earl of Wemyss (where Chalmers Hospital stands) and Ramsay Lodge (the site of the Art College and the Fire Brigade HQ) gradually disappeared.

GEORGE WATSON'S HOSPITAL

On the sloping ground to the north of the Burgh Loch was another charitable institution – the hospital built by the legacy of George Watson, who died in 1723. Among other positions in his professional life, he was accountant to the Bank of Scotland, and the bulk of his estate was entrusted to the Merchant Company to carry out his wishes of creating a hospital school for boys, the children and grandchildren of 'decayed' merchants. Watson also left money to the Merchant Maiden, Trades Maiden and Heriot's Hospitals.

It was 1738 before the hospital governors feued seven acres of land from Heriot's Hospital, and in 1741 the hospital, designed by William Adam, was ready to receive its first ten foundationers.

Designed by William Adam of the renowned architectural family, building of George Watson's Hospital started in 1738 on a site overlooking the Meadows. It was originally for orphan boys. When the Royal Infirmary moved to Lauriston Place in the 19th century, Watson's Hospital building was incorporated into it. The school then moved to nearby Archibald Place and in 1930 to its present location in Colinton Road, where it is now co-educational.

They appeared to be heartily fed from the start, and they were supplied with a uniform which elicited the comment that the pupils were made to look 'more, in all respects, like the sons of gentlemen, than charity children'.

One of the early entrants to the hospital was James Craig, who would be the designer of the first New Town.

A description of the Adam building in J. and H.S. Storer's *Views in Edinburgh and its Vicinity* reads:

> It presents a handsome and extensive front to the northwards composed of two slightly projecting wings, and a centre surmounted by a low spire having a ship on its summit as an emblem of merchandise; against the roof of this part of the building is raised a large tablet of stone, richly ornamented, with armorial buildings; the elevation of the centre is also assisted by an additional storey, which occasions an agreeable and judicious break in the otherwise continuous line of the roof. In front of the Hospital is an extensive piece of ground for the exercise of the scholars, who wear uniform dress, consisting of a dark-coloured jacket and trowsers.

The hospital, with later extensions, was converted to a day school in 1870, but the following year it had to move into the Merchant Maiden building in nearby Archibald Place because the Royal Infirmary had approached the governors to buy the original building to allow a move from its own crowded Infirmary Street site. The new infirmary in Lauriston Place incorporated Watson's Hospital into the new medical hospital, and the Royal Infirmary chapel was substantially the Watson's chapel of the 1858 west wing extension.

The old Infirmary was demolished in 1884, although the former surgical hospital building remains in Drummond Street.

Watson's stayed in the Archibald Place building, which was acquired by the Infirmary for expansion in 1926, until 1932, when it moved to Colinton Road and where the co-educational George Watson's College presently thrives, with the bright 'emblem of merchandise,' the ship which is part of the Merchant Company's symbol, still soaring over the building.

With the Royal Infirmary moving to a greenfield site at Little France, the Royal Infirmary buildings in Lauriston Place are now in the throes of a major redevelopment which will see much of the Victorian construction retained, and other buildings making way for 21st-century structures.

CHAPTER 7

CONFLAGRATION

Wrichtis-housis was only one of the ancient and historical buildings to be lost in the 19th century, which was to see clearances on a hitherto unprecedented scale.

Partly this was because new roads had to be formed; partly it was because, yet again, houses were ruinous; partly there seemed to be no sense of the need for conservation; and partly it was done for the best of reasons – to provide better housing for people trapped in appalling conditions. And finally it was because the feared enemy of Edinburgh over the years, not the English this time, but fire, once again struck with devastating force.

Spectacular blazes seemed to occur regularly in the early 1800s, starting with one on 8 January in the first year of the century. On that occasion the Edinburgh Sugar House in the Canongate was razed and its materials and utensils destroyed.

The following year, the Lochrin Distillery granary near Tollcross was found to be on fire. 'The fire engines attended immediately; but though every possible exertion was made, the whole was burnt down. The whole was, however, insured,' says a contemporay report.

The premises of Francis Braidwood, an upholsterer in the Pleasance, were 'entirely consumed' in November 1807.

Early in the morning of Sunday, 10 November 1811, fire destroyed a great part of the Exchequer Chamber in Parliament Square, endangering the adjoining buildings.

'Very great exertions being made to quench the flames, they were at length got under, though not before all the upper part of the building was destroyed,' Chambers reports. 'The fire was so strong, and the night so favourable for its appearance, that, to a distant beholder from the south, it seemed as if the whole of the Parliament Square were in one blaze.'

A 'most destructive and memorable fire' erupted in the fourth storey of

Bishop's Land, at the head of Carrubber's Close, on the north side of the High Street in 1813. The land (or tenement) was at that time one of the most substantial and attractive private buildings in the length of the street. On its ground floor was an arched arcade or piazza, supported by stout stone piers. At one time it was the home of John Spottiswood, Archbishop of St Andrews, who inherited it from his father, and the date 1578 was on the stonework.

'So aristocratic were the denizens of this once fashionable tenement,' observes Wilson, 'that we have been told by an old citizen there was not a family resident in any its flats who did not keep livery servants: a strange contrast to their plebian succcessors.'

The fire which destroyed the splendid tenement was said to have started in the home of a family who were at Sunday evening worship.

The fire trail continued unabated.

In 1818 three flats in the West Bow were destroyed and ten families lost their homes.

In 1819 a 'very destructive' blaze broke out in a row of shops on the east side of North Bridge. It was in the small hours of 5 March and the alarm was raised at three o'clock.

'In spite of every exertion, the whole premises were levelled with the ground at five,' says Chambers.

The buildings being very old, principally of wood, and only two storeys in height, fell an easy prey to the flames. They were part of the houses in the Cap and Feather Close, which, with the exception of them, was completely removed to make way for the North Bridge, on the extension of the Royalty in 1767. They had obstinately kept their place there, to the disgust of all who took an interest in the appearance of this city, till fire at length rid the Magistrates of their grievous eye-sore, and made way for the handsome and uniform tenements which now (1824) occupy their place.

A feeling mind could scarcely part with them, however old and ugly as they were, without regret; for they formed the last relics of the close in which the ingenious but unfortunate bard, Robert Fergusson, was born.

OPPOSITE.

The Parliament Stairs, also known as the Back Stairs and the Meal Market Stairs, made a steep access from Parliament Close to the Cowgate. In the changes in the area after the 1824 fire, the stairs trodden by generations of Edinburghers were removed.

In 1821 a fire about midnight in the second storey of a house in the Cowgate opposite the Parliament Stairs (which descended from the Parliament Square into the lower street) had more tragic results.

'The stair, unfortunately a wooden one, very soon caught fire and cut off the escape of a poor family in the fourth flat, consisting of father, mother and three children, who took the desperate resolution of leaping from the windows into the street,' Chambers relates.

> The father, with one child in his arms, escaped with a few bruises; but the mother, who first threw over one child, which was saved, and then jumped down the dreadful height with another in her arms, was not so fortunate. She was so severely hurt that she expired a short time after in the Infirmary. A boy, also a member of this hapless family, in jumping over, was likewise killed. This calamitous fire was supposed to have been occasioned by the imprudence of a convivial party in the second flat, who had met at a christening.

Another fatal incident occurred in September 1822, when fire broke out in an old wooden tenement at the corner of Lady Wynd at the foot of the West Port.

> This house, which was burnt to the ground, had long been a common resort of lodgers of the lowest description, and exhibited a small placard under one of its windows, with 'Beds to Let' written upon it, referring to wretched lairs, let, we understand, at twopence per night. A great number of wretches were turned out naked into the streets; but in one of the rooms, a poor Irish labourer and two children were unhappily burnt to death.
>
> One person was roused by some neighbour-lodger, on the first alarm, and could scarcely be dragged from his pallet. He had paid his twopence, he said, and was determined to have his sleep out. However, he was eventually roused, and brought away.

OPPOSITE.

The Great Fire of November 1824 left a large part of Parliament Close and the south side of the High Street below St Giles' devastated. Many tenements were destroyed and some of the buildings had to be pulled down because they were in a dangerous state after the flames consumed the area between the High Street and the Cowgate. As a result of the fire, one of several that year, Edinburgh's fire brigade, which was in the course of being set up, was speedily confirmed under the direction of James Braidwood, becoming the first municipal fire brigade in the world.

But it was 1824, which brought a catalogue of house fires, culminating in the Great Fire, which caused more damage to the town than any seen since it was laid waste by the English.

A large printing house in Niddry Street, off the High Street, had been destroyed; then one of the new buildings on North Bridge was virtually gutted.

One 24 June, fire started in a 'tippling-house' (tavern) at the head of Royal Bank Close and its ferocity destroyed the tenement above. Then flames spread to the adjacent house 'and did not stop till it had demolished the half of the east side of Parliament Square.'

Water had to be sprayed on the smoking ruins for four days, but despite the extensive damage only one man died from burns he received while trying to rescue some Council papers from an office.

'This fire was considered the most extensive and destructive that had happened since that of 1700; but another shortly after occured in its immediate neighbourhood, which surpassed both of these,' Chambers says.

This was the Great Fire of Edinburgh.

On the night of 15 November the alarm was raised when smoke was seen pouring from a second-floor flat at the head of Old Assembly Close. Despite the best efforts of the firefighters, the fires spread and another two tenements were soon alight. Because of the narrowness of the close it was impossible to get the fire-engines near, and within 90 minutes of the first alarm, three tenements were engulfed as the fire ripped through flat after flat and business premises. The fire spread down the closes towards the Cowgate, the back tenements of Borthwick's and the Old Assembly Closes being 'entirely consumed'.

After 11 or 12 hours, the fire was pretty much under control. Then the sparks were blown onto the Tron Kirk, and a desperate effort was made by the firemen to save it. The old Dutch spire with its weathercock fell with a tremendous crash into the street and the bulk of the building was spared further damage.

But worse was yet to come. At 10 o'clock on the Tuesday night, a new alarm was raised; fire had broken out in 'the immense pile' – 11 storeys high – on the south side of Parliament Square.

'This was a perfectly distinct conflagration,' Chambers states, 'and had the effect of impressing people with an idea that Heaven was beginning to afflict them with a series of terrific and destructive calamities.'

It spread quickly down towards the Cowgate and to houses on the east side of the square, which were soon 'one huge burning tower'.

The Parliament Square and St Giles' resounded with awful echoes;

the torches of the firemen below threw up a horrid light upon the tall surrounding buildings; and as the flames proceeded, volumes of smoke and embers were driven eastward in violent and appalling career across the Old Town.

Sparks were again soaring into the air, and they set fire to buildings in the rear of the High Street. Throughout the next days, small fires started in house chimneys as burning embers were carried on the wind.

Some 400 people were driven from their homes with whatever possessions they could rescue, and one old woman blamed the calamity as a judgment on the recent music festival in the town!

The final 'extent of the mischief', is described by Chambers:

Along the front of the High Street there were destroyed four lands of six storeys each, beside the sunk storeys; from there down towards the Cowgate by Conn's Close, two wooden lands; in the Old Assembly Close, four lands of six or seven storeys; six smaller tenements in Borthwick's Close; four lands of six storeys in the Old Fishmarket Close.

Downwards, nearly as far as the Cowgate, nothing was to be seen but frightful heaps of ruin, to which all approach was rendered highly dangerous, by the walls which were left standing in different places, but in an extremely tottering condition.

Along the front of the Parliament Square, four double lands, of from seven to 11 storeys each, were destroyed.

Much of the still-standing damaged property was pulled down for safety. The blaze cemented the already mooted formation of a municipal fire brigade – the first in the world – under the direction of James Braidwood.

That fire caused the loss of much of old Edinburgh, necessitating the rebuilding of most of the south side of the High Street from St Giles' down to the Tron. The Parliament Square south side was reserved for the construction of a new court complex beside Parliament House.

CHAPTER 8
BOWED OUT

The next big change came with the scheme prepared by Thomas Hamilton under the Improvement Act of 1827 to create a new western approach beneath the Castle rock to join the Lawnmarket at its junction with Castlehill and the top of the West Bow, site of the former western entrance into early Edinburgh.

WEST BOW

The Bow was a z-shaped lane which connected the Lawnmarket to the Grassmarket and contained some of the oldest houses in the city. The wooden outshoots from the buildings above street level were at some points so close to each other 'as to admit the inhabitants interchanging the pleasure of tea drinking, without the trouble of leaving their respective abodes'.

The Bow was destroyed when Victoria Street and Victoria Terrace were constructed between 1829–34, giving access to the new George IV Bridge, which was part of the new southern route envisaged in the improvements. There is still a small section of houses dating from the late 17th century at the foot of the Bow, just below where it was merged with Victoria Street, but there is now no sign of places such as the Old Assembly Room, with the date of 1602 and the Somerville arms inscribed on it. Here took place the early assemblies (or dances), run under almost martinet control by a mistress of ceremonies.

OPPOSITE.

The head of the West Bow, looking up Castlehill. The steep z-shaped lane of the West Bow led from the top of the Lawnmarket to the Grassmarket and contained the houses of many eminent citizens over the years. The construction of Victoria Street and Victoria Terrace between 1829 and 1834 ripped the heart out of the historic thoroughfare and saw the end of many old houses. At the foot of the Bow today are buildings which can be dated to the 17th century.

The dance hall was in the house on the west side of the narrow lane, at the first angle of the Bow down from the Lawnmarket, and the building was probably erected by Bailie Peter Somerville. It is believed to have been the last within James II's city wall, and the iron hook on which the Bow port had swung was impaled for many years in its wall.

When the poet Oliver Goldsmith stayed in Edinburgh in 1753 as a medical student, he was able to provide a description of just how an evening of dance was conducted.

> Let me say something of their balls, which are very frequent here. When a stranger enters the dancing-hall, he sees one end of the room taken up with the ladies, who sit dismally in a group by themselves; on the other end stand their pensive partners that are to be; but no more intercourse between the sexes than between two countries at war. The ladies, indeed, may ogle and the gentlemen sigh, but an embargo is laid upon any closer commerce. At length, to interrupt hostilities, the lady-directress, intendant, or what you will, pitches on a gentleman and a lady to walk a minuet, which they perform with a formality approaching to despondence. After five or six couples have thus walked the gauntlet, all stand up to country dances, each gentleman furnished with a partner from the aforesaid lady-directress. So they dance much, and say nothing, and thus concludes our Assembly.

MAJOR WEIR'S HOUSE

Opposite the Assembly Room, which was demolished in 1836, stood the courtyard entrance into one of the most frightening houses in the town – if local gossip and legends are to be believed. It belonged to the notorious Major Thomas Weir, 'The Wizard of the Bow', whose claim to infamy was that he was regarded as being in league with the Devil. Indeed, his sister Grizel, or Jean, who shared the house, declared that Satan's coach had come to the house to collect them and take them to Dalkeith, south of the town.

The end of a complicated story came when Weir, who had won wide respect as a former professional soldier who had served as a Captain of the

OPPOSITE.
The West Bow Assembly Room, where strict rules were enforced for dancing.

City Guard and as a lay preacher with a congregation which met regularly in his home, was finally put on trial in April 1670. He confessed to what Wilson calls 'possible and impossible' crimes. They included incest with his sister. He was sentenced to be strangled and burned at the stake – the punishment for those convicted of dealings with the devil. He died at the Gallowlea, between Edinburgh and Leith, crying out, 'I have lived as a beast, and I must die as a beast.'

Grizel, who, it was generally accepted, was mentally unhinged, died the day after her brother on the scaffold in the Grassmarket.

The house then lay deserted and rapidly gained a reputation for being haunted by the Weirs. Locals told of seeing the Major appear at midnight on a headless horse which clattered from the courtyard entrance and galloped off down the Bow. The house, understandably, had no takers keen to share the abode with any ghosts, until one brave couple eventually said they would live there – but they stayed only one night. They were wakened in their bed by a noise, only to see a calf-like creature at the foot of the bed.

The building was eventually used as a store, with, it was said, no one in more than two centuries again daring to stay overnight. It was spared in the Improvements to sweep through the Bow but was demolished later in the century.

Another fine house was that belonging to Lord Provost Archibald Stewart, who reputedly entertained Bonnie Prince Charlie there in 1745, when the Highlanders had occupied the town, and, it is said, smuggled him out of a secret passage to safety when troops from the Castle, still held by Government forces, were tipped off that they might entrap their enemy as he dined with Stewart.

The house, occupied at one time by an eminent watchmaker, Paul Romieu, was demolished in 1835, while the timber-fronted Mahoganay Land survived only a further few years before it, too, was lost for ever. Yet another fine property, that owned by Alexander Donaldson, the book-seller and founder of the *Edinburgh Advertiser*, which had been unoccupied for some years, burned down.

The zeal with which the improvers set about their task was frightening in its intensity not to let anything – least of all the town's architectural history –

OPPOSITE.

The most feared house in the West Bow was that once occupied by Major Thomas Weir and his sister Grizel, convicted and executed for their admitted involvement with the devil and carnal offences in 17th-century Edinburgh. It was near the top of the Bow.

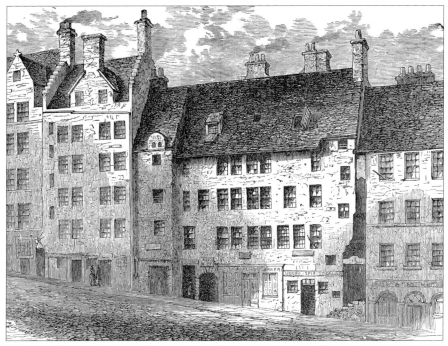

Major Weir's Land attracted the curiosity of citizens and visitors alike, and was eventually demolished later in the 19th century, by which time many of the other old properties in the thoroughfare were already gone.

OPPOSITE.

The narrow timber-fronted Mahogany Land in the West Bow was typical of the building style there, with a business on the ground floor and a stairway leading to the upper levels. In the adjoining tenement is another common feature, the stone arcade, similar to that which can still be seen in Gladstone's Land in the Lawnmarket.

stand in their way. 'Various ancient closes, and very picturesque front lands that formed the continuation of the southern side of the Castlehill were swept away to give place to the new western approach and the Assembly Hall,' comments Wilson. That hall, known for many years as the Highland Tolbooth Church, is now the Hub, base of the Edinburgh International Festival Society, and was built between 1839–44.

One of the places swept away was Ross's Court, where the Marquis of Argyle had his house in Castlehill, referred to by William Creech in his *Fugitive Pieces* as being inhabited in the 1780s. Another was Kennedy's Close, whose front land was thought to have been at one time the town mansion of the Earl of Cassillis.

Mary of Guise and Lorraine was the widow of James V, mother of Mary, Queen of Scots, and Regent of Scotland from 1554 to 1560. It is believed her 'palace' was built at the top of the Lawnmarket to provide a safe refuge within the city walls in the 1540s. Originally it had an ornate interior and garden grounds sloping to the Nor' Loch behind. The much altered building was demolished in 1861 when the Free Church Assembly Hall was created.

MARY OF GUISE PALACE

In the same section of the Royal Mile, at the point where the Castlehill merges on the north side of the street with the Lawnmarket was the house known as the Palace of Mary of Guise, on the west side of Blyth's Close. Despite its associations with Queen Mary, the widow of James V, Queen Regent from 1554 to 1560 and mother of the infant Mary, Queen of Scots, the 'palace' was demolished in 1845 to clear the site for the Free Church Assembly Hall. In the latter building the reconvened Scottish Parliament met before moving in 2004 to its new home at Holyrood.

The palace building stretched over three closes – Blyth's, Todd's and Nairn's – and from contemporary reports and examination at the time of demolition was ornately decorated, with many fine wooden panels. The house was created to provide a safe refuge within the city walls for the Queen Regent in tumultuous times, and the property contained not only living quarters but

The Mary of Guise Palace in the Lawnmarket was a grand building spreading over several closes and included an oratory for private worship for the mother of Mary, Queen of Scots. A substantial building, it was also a stronghold for her and her household during her regency for her daughter.

also reception rooms and an oratory. One chamber in the palace was called the 'deid-room', where any member of the royal establishment who passed away was laid out between death and burial. Like some other old houses in Edinburgh, it also had a hidden chamber on the first floor. Lit by a narrow slit into Nairn's Close, the entrance to this room was by a movable wooden panel and provided access to a flight of stairs. Thus, visitors might make an

Old Bank Close, with its attractive houses, was one of the picturesque corners to vanish with the construction of George IV Bridge. The Bank of Scotland moved to new headquarters at the top of the Mound.

unheralded entrance into the palace, and its inhabitants had the reassurance of a hidden escape route.

The rich internal decoration of the palace and its chapel made it at one time the finest of all in Edinburgh, its huge stone mantelpieces in the principal apartments having pillared supports. There were also two carved oak mantelpieces in two of the oratory rooms with figures of the four Evangelists.

Originally, a garden stretched northwards towards the banks of the Nor' Loch. In later times the site of the upper garden ground was occupied by a brushmaker's workshops and yard, while the lower area was covered by the Earthern Mound of rubble excavated for the foundations of the buildings in the first New Town. The building itself was, like so many of the Old Town's once stately homes, divided into small apartments before its demolition.

Robert Gourlay's House

Another very substantial mansion which was lost under the Improvement Act was Robert Gourlay's House, standing in Old Bank Close, which was more or less on the western side of Melbourne Place, the start of George IV Bridge. The

Another casualty of the development of George IV Bridge in the 19th century was Robert Gourlay's House, which stood on the site of the present Melbourne Place. It was one of the biggest and sturdiest of the old Edinburgh houses, and at one time prisoners were held in it.

house was built in 1569 by Robert Gourlay, a town merchant, on the site of an old religious house, and carried the inscription 'O Lord in thee is all my trust' – and was strong enough to be used as a place of confinement for prominent prisoners. It also had a secret chamber, between the ceiling of the first and floor of the second storey, discovered only when the house was demolished.

Gourlay was an elder in the reformed St Giles' and was 'ordained to make his public repentance in the church for transporting wheat out of the country'.

The Bank of Scotland resided in the close from 1700 until moving to its new headquarters at the top of the Mound in 1806. Bank Street itself was created in 1798, cutting through the closes in this section of the Lawnmarket.

Before the new street opened, pedestrians slipped down Lady Stair's Close to reach the then half-formed mound which was a link across the valley to the expanding New Town.

The Improvements Commissioners were urged to preserve the Gourlay House because of its 'interesting fabric' and its associations with national figures and events, but the pleas were ignored because of its position close to the line of the new bridge and the fact that it was 'little adapted to modern requirements, and not unnaturally failed to commend itself to city reformers'.

GOSFORD'S CLOSE

Close by in Gosford's Close, obliterated in 1835, stood a timber-fronted land with a sculptured and inscribed 16th-century lintel. The demolition men found in its lower regions a stout arched cellar, with a trapdoor leading to another underground room, possibly used by smugglers who secreted their contraband after hauling it across the Nor' Loch. The vault still lies beneath George IV Bridge, according to Wilson.

LIBBERTON'S WYND

The formation of George IV Bridge to span the Cowgate and Merchant Street meant the demolition of several old closes, among them Libberton's Wynd, a steep, picturesque passageway mentioned as far back as 1474. For Edinburgh citizens, when it was taken away, however, memories of the ancient thoroughfare, at one time one of the main approaches from the once fashionable Cowgate to the foot of the Lawnmarket, would have centred on one of the town's best known hostelries. Johnny Dowie's Tavern, previously the Mermaid, was the meeting place of 'the chief wits and men of letters' in the 18th century. Here, figures such as the poet Robert Fergusson, author Henry Mackenzie, Court of Session judges and many other distinguished men would gather to drink, eat and discuss the worthy matters of the day.

OPPOSITE.
Libberton's Wynd, first mentioned as far back as 1474, ran from the bottom of the Lawnmarket southwards to the Cowgate. It was a steep, picturesque passageway proving a vital link for the citizens between the two principal streets. At its head was the execution spot, marked today by three brass studs on the pavement at the George IV Bridge and Lawnmarket junction. The wynd itself was finally removed with the construction of the bridge.

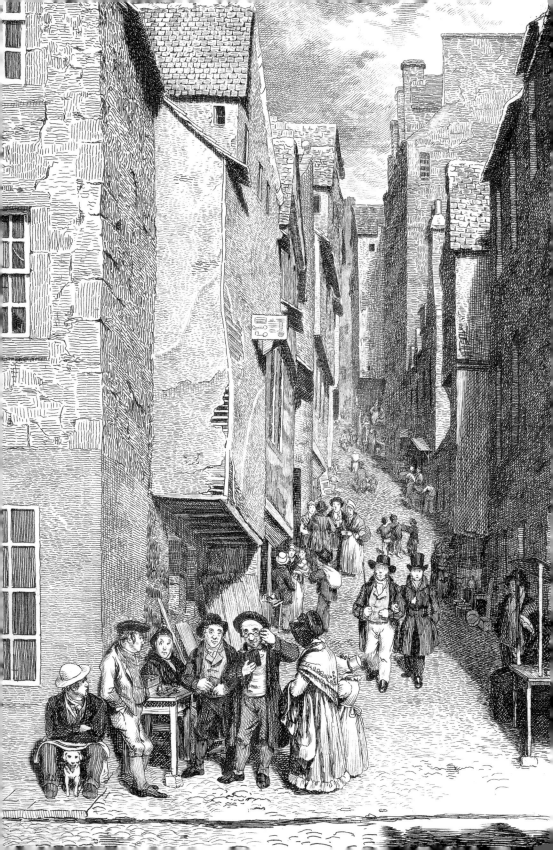

A great proportion of this house was literally without light, consisting of a series of windowless chambers, decreasing in size till the last was a mere box, of irregular oblong figure, jocularly, but not inappropriately designated the Coffin,' reports Chambers. 'Besides these, there were but two rooms possessing light, and as that came from a deep, narrow alley, it was light little more than in name. Hither, nevertheless, did many of the Parliament House men come daily for their meridian [the mid-day dram]. Here nightly assembled companies of cits [citizens], as well as men of wit and of fashion, to spend hours in what may, by comparison, be described as gentle conviviality.

One of Dowie's most popular drinks was Younger's Edinburgh Ale – 'a potent fluid which almost glued the lips of the drinker together, and of which few, therefore, could dispatch more than a bottle'. He also offered pub grub – 'a bit of toasted cheese, a crumb of tripe, ham, a dish o' pease'.

The poet Robert Burns almost inevitably found his way there, and the pub in its later life was called Burns' Tavern. The building bore the date 1728, and the wynd was one of the few to keep its name throughout its existence, it being common practice for the inhabitant of the largest house in a close to name it after himself.

Libberton's Wynd finally went in 1834, but at the head of the old lane at the foot of the Lawnmarket until 1864 public hangings took place. After the demolition of the Old Tolbooth, another execution site was needed. While George Bryce earned the distinction of being the last man hanged before the public view, the largest and most excitable crowd turned out in 1829 to see the serial killer William Burke go to the gallows. His partner in crime, William Hare, escaped execution by turning King's Evidence and testifying against his fellow Irishman. The names of Burke and Hare are inextricably linked in the infamy of Edinburgh's past.

Three brass studs set into the pavement opposite the High Court building in the Lawnmarket mark the former execution spot.

So many of the old closes were swept away in the various redevelopments

OPPOSITE.
Libberton's Wynd was renowned as the home of one of the town's most popular pubs – Johnny Dowie's Tavern, later called Burns' Tavern because the Scottish bard frequented the hostelry on his visits to Edinburgh. In the partially subterranean rooms, leading citizens were happy to pass many an hour with good company, fine food and ample ale and other drinks, catching up on the local gossip.

Jenny Ha's (Janet Hall's) tavern in the Canongate was typical, offering food and drink and being particularly renowned for its claret. John Gay, who wrote 'The Beggar's Opera', frequented the alehouse and mingled with other literary men. Many of the taverns were presided over by strong-willed, yet sympathetic, women known as 'luckies'. Some of them were immortalised in the 18th-century poems of Allan Ramsay and Robert Fergusson. The modernised Jenny Ha's public house in the Canongate changed its historic name in 2011.

– places such as Carthrae's or Turk's, Forrester's and Beth's Wynds stood on the area between Libberton's Wynd and St Giles' at one time – 'but every vestige of them had been swept away before the later work of destruction was projected,' says Wilson.

Before George IV Bridge was built, however, a fine building had appeared on part of Libberton's Wynd – the Midlothian County Hall. Designed by Archibald Eliott and executed by John Inglis, it was on the north-west corner of Parliament Square. In 1818 the Michaelmas Head Court was held for the first time in its courtroom.

'The exterior of the building eastward is ornamented with a beautiful portico; the pediment is suppoorted by four fluted columns with finely carved capitals, and the entrance is ascended to by a handsome flight of stairs. This splendid building is a great improvement to the High Streeet, particularly as the old and dreary prison of the Tolbooth has been taken down during the

Midlothian County Hall was up and running in 1818 and part of Libberton's Wynd was demolished to make way for it. In time the County Hall was replaced between 1900 and 1905 by the Midlothian County Council building, now part of the City Council's Royal Mile presence, on the corner of the Lawnmarket and George IV Bridge.

period of its erection; other beneficial alterations are likewise in progress in its immediate neighbourhood: the shops which obstructed the south side of St Giles' Cathedral are removed, and a complete reparation of the church is intended ...' runs a contemporary report.

The hall was replaced between 1900–05 by the Midlothian County Council Building, designed by J. Macintyre Henry, later the Lothian Region Chambers, and is still in the possession of the City Council. On the east frontage of the building are striking friezes featuring agriculture, mining and fishing.

CHAPTER 9

DESTRUCTION

COWGATE

The impact of the 1827 Improvement Act was inevitably felt on the other major street in the Old Town – the Cowgate. With the closes running down from the southern slopes of the High Street, it was obvious that demolition of property there would be required for the proposed George IV Bridge. Known as the 'New-street' or 'South-gait', the Cowgait was recorded as early as 1335.

The Scots word 'gait' (gate) was applied to a way or route, not necessarily to an opening gate, and in the Cowgate were many springs and wells which provided a water supply for householders and an ample source for the alemakers. In 1592 it was described as the place 'where the nobility and chief men of the city reside and in which are the palaces of the officers of state, and where nothing is mean and tasteless but all is magnificent'.

By the 19th century, it was the scene of some of the worst slums in the city, and with that, together with the formation of George IV Bridge and the earlier South Bridge across the valley to the south of the High Street, the seeds of the virtual destruction of the old Cowgate were sewn.

'Indeed, if we except the old mint and the venerable Chapel of St Magdalene, no other site could have been chosen for the new (George IV) bridge where their proceedings would have been so destructive,' wrote Wilson sadly:

> On the ground where the bridge's southern piers were built stood Merchant's Court, a large area enclosed on three sides by antique buildings in a plain but massive style of architecture, containing internally finely stuccoed ceilings and handsome panelling with other indications of former magnificance.

It had been the mansion of Thomas Hamilton, the first Earl of Haddington, a

The Cowgate suffered a terrible slump from being one of the finest living areas to a virtual slum in the 19th century. The clearance programme meant that most of the ancient houses were pulled down, and little remains of the distinctive architecture which once graced the street.

favourite of James VI and one of the most eminent men of his time. 'Tam o' the Cowgate' was the king's name for him and his being in that street confirms that it was, in its prime, the best address in old Edinburgh.

The ground appears to have been first granted by James III to Lord Bothwell in 1485, passing through various hands until it came into the possession of Hamilton, who was President of the Court of Session and Secretary of State for Scotland. The house courtyard formed three sides of a square entering from the Cowgate through a pend or arched passage adjoining the Magdalene Chapel and had another outlet to Candlemaker Row behind.

Hamilton died in 1637 and in 1691 the property was bought by the Merchant Company, whose name was transferred to the court. It was here that the Merchant Maiden Hospital had its first premises before moving to Bristo. A portion of the court was later leased to the Commissioners of Excise for an office. The Merchant Company bought ground on the west side of Hunter

Square for a new Merchant Hall (now in Hanover Street) and the old court was let to various parties before it was sold off to the Commissioners of Improvement in 1829 and soon pulled down for the construction of the bridge.

FRENCH AMBASSADOR'S CHAPEL

Opposite the Hamilton Mansion and at the foot of Libberton's Wynd was what was called the French Ambassador's Chapel, a designation dating back to Queen Mary's time, when there was a French embassy in the Cowgate. A good example of a Scottish semi-fortified house with a strong square tower, resembling a Borders peel, the highest storey of the west wing was decorated with the carved heads of the Twelve Apostles. There was also said to be the stone figure of Jesus above, but the upper part of the body was broken off.

Also called the 'Twelve Apostles' House', it was built originally by John Dickison of Winkston, who was murdered in broad daylight in Peebles High Street in 1572.

Behind the chapel building was the huge tenement where the author Henry Mackenzie was born. It was also destroyed during the building of George IV Bridge in 1829.

HOPE MANSION

It is appropriate while in the part of the Cowgate beneath the bridge to mention another well-known house which would vanish later in the century. This was the mansion of Sir Thomas Hope, who was King's Advocate to Charles I, and the house is dated to 1616. A detailed description gives a good impression of what a really wealthy man could build – 'that great Lodging or tenement of land, high and laigh, back and forth, under and above', as the earliest document in Latin referes to the house. It had two doorways from the streeet and an arched entrance into its courtyard.

The house became known as Hopetoun Land after Sir Thomas's death in

OPPOSITE.

The Cowgate contained many distinguished houses. The French Ambassador's House or Chapel, removed in 1829, stood on the north side of the street, close to the foot of Libberton's Wynd, and was decorated with carvings of the Twelve Apostles' heads. The property's name relates to the time of Mary, Queen of Scots, when an envoy from France was resident in Scotland. It was on the line of George IV Bridge support works. At that time many old properties were cleared to make way for the new road to the south which soars over the Cowgate from the heart of the Royal Mile.

1646. After passing through several hands, it was purchased in 1758 by the Corporation of Baxters (bakers of Edinburgh), who built barns and a malthouse in its garden grounds and also in the garden area of another distinguished house once held by the Littles of Libberton, which stretched upwards north behind the Hope Mansion. By the 19th century this was sub-divided, part of it being a lodging house and inn.

The site was cleared between 1887–90 for the Central Public Library, which soars from the Cowgate well above the level of George IV Bridge. Two dorway lintels from Sir Thomas Hope's house are incorporated into the library.

It was the vision of a New Town and its development on the countryside to the north, together with steady building on the south, that led to the demise of the Old Town on the ridge. The old mansions and tenements came to be more and more sub-divided as their former owners moved out, attracted by a new style of spacious living in the burgeoning northern and southern suburbs as the town burst out from its old boundaries.

A visitor to the city in 1774–5, Captain Edward Topham, makes a wry observation about the early days of the New Town:

> The greater part of the New Town is built after the manner of the English, and the houses are what they call here 'houses to themselves' … yet such is the force of prejudice that there are many people who prefer a little dark confined tenement on the sixth floor, to the convenience of a whole house. One lady fancies she would be lost to go to such a habitation; another, that she would be blown away in going over the new (North) bridge; and a third lives in the old style, because she is sure that these new fashions can come to 'nae gude'.

As the population steadily increased – in 1800 it was about 80,000, by 1827 about 120,000 and in 1840 the figure was near the 140,000 mark, with a flood of immigrants descending on the town from the Highlands and later from Ireland – the once douce tenement stairs reeked with the problems of over-occupation and its attendant poverty, squalor and neglect.

It was particularly rank in what had become the dingiest of slums in parts

OPPOSITE.

The last days of Hope Mansion, once one of the grandest of all the homes in the Cowgate.
Latterly it was a lodging house and its end came when its site was cleared to make way for the
Central Library, designed by G. Washington Browner and built between 1887 and 1890.
The library's public entrance is on George IV Bridge.

of the High Street, Cowgate, the Canongate and around the Grassmarket, where the housing conditions were at their worst and causing concern to at least some socially minded citizens.

HEAVE AWA'

An example of what could so easily happen if the structure of a building was allowed to deteriorate occurred with dramatic unexpectedness one November night in 1861. A tenement in the High Street below North Bridge 'ran together with a hideous uproar and tumbled down storey upon storey to the ground'. In all, 35 inhabitants died in the calamity. The event is recorded on the carving on the Bailie Fyfe's Close tenement, which was built on the site. It reads: 'Heave awa' chaps, I'm no deid yet!' reputedly the cry from a young lad trapped in the rubble to his rescuers.

The pressure of public protest led to the appointment of Dr Henry Littlejohn to the new post of Medical Officer of Health for the town. He speedily carried out a survey into the sanitary conditions about which churchmen such as Dr Thomas Guthrie and Dr William Chalmers, and concerned laymen and medical men, spoke publicly and wrote.

Dr George Bell had published a pamphlet in 1850 in which he wrote: 'We return day after day and night after night to the scenes of misery, disease and death; we listen to the cry of children, the wail of women and the deep utterances of men.' He described the conditions he found in Blackfriars' Wynd – where there was not a drop of water, except in one comparatively new tenement at the top of the street. There was no drain in the wynd 'and consequently all the filth of the place remains on the surface'.

A survey a year earlier had shown 597 men, women and children living in the wynd, but Dr Bell found 1,025 in the 142 buildings there, containing 198 chambers. One older woman was living in a room barely 6 feet square, with a small skylight and no fireplace – 'The floor is full of holes and the walls are creviced, and it is such a place as an owl might inhabit for the sake of the mice and other prey which have an interest here. There is not a stick of furniture in the chamber.'

A series of hard-hitting articles in the *Evening Courant* had exposed the ever worsening conditions in which people were condemned to exist and

OPPOSITE.
One of the doorways to Hope Mansion was preserved and incorporated into the Central Library.

added further fuel to the demands for action to be taken to clear the slums.

Dr Littlejohn's own *Report on the Sanitary Conditions of the City of Edinburgh 1865* gave the Town Council a detailed description of close after close in the High Street, Canongate, Grassmarket, West Port, the Pleasance, St Leonard's and other districts, leaving no doubt that something had to be done. A year earlier the Council had taken powers to enforce the introduction of WCs into the houses of the poor.

But the driving zeal came from William Chambers when he became Lord Provost in 1865. He secured the Improvement Act of 1867 to acquire property to be rebuilt and brought the creation of new streets: namely, Market Street, Cranston Street, Jeffrey Street, Chambers Street, Guthrie Street, Lady Lawson Street, Marshall Street and Howden Street. It meant, of course, that a large slice of picturesque Old Town tenements were lost and closes were irretrievably carved up, as had happened when (Lord) Cockburn Street was formed in an earlier improvement in 1856 to provide a link from the High Street to Waverley Station, which was by then in the valley of the old Nor' Loch.

The Improvement Act of 1867 finally put a nail in the coffin of the Cowgate, already carved up by the piers and adjoining structures of the two bridges. Among the houses now to be lost were timber-fronted houses along the main frontage, together with those in Bull's Close.

CARDINAL BEATON'S HOUSE

At the foot of Blackfriars' Wynd stood Cardinal Beaton's House or Palace, with its distinctive hexagonal turret. It was another complex of once-fine elegant buildings stretching up the wynd and fronting the main street, and was one of the finest of all the Cowgate properties.

It housed royal guests on occasions, including James V, and it may have been the temporary home of the town's grammar school when the Council rented property in 1555 while the new High School was being built not far distant.

The palace entrance was from Blackfriars Wynd, and a flight of broad stairs led to the first floor with the principal rooms. The under flat was arched

OPPOSITE.

This timber-fronted house in the Cowgate may look eye-catching, but to the poor folk forced to live here in the second half of the 19th century the building would have been damp, insanitary, overcrowded and putrid. Houses like these were rented off by landlords who took as much income as possible, and spent little, if anything, on a house's maintenance.

over with masonry, and when the house was taken down in 1874 it was found that the space between the arches and the floor above was packed with quarry sand, which would help to make the stone-built house almost fireproof. The gardens in Beaton's time extended over the ground afterwards covered by the Scottish Mint buildings.

Inevitably, after it passed out of ecclesiatical use, the palace and its associated buildings fell into other hands and were put to different purposes. In the last quarter of the 18th century, for instance, in the house and under the sign of the Golden Cock, was a shop belonging to the last of the traditional lorimers who made the ironwork used by saddlers.

But something of the status of the wynd can be found from an advertisement which appeared in April 1703 in the *Evening Courant*. It read: 'There is a boarding-school to be set up in Blackfriars' Wynd, in Robinson's Land, upon the west side of the Wynd, near the middle thereof, in the first door of the stair leading to the said land, against the latter end of May, or first of June next, when young ladies and gentlemen may have all sorts of breeding that is to be had in any parts of Britain, and great care taken of their conversation.'

It would probably still have been an elegant address at that time, but a different picture emerges in the 1860s. Willian Anderson, a reporter on the *Evening Courant,* wrote a series of accounts for the newspaper on the slums of Edinburgh as he found them in 1866 and 1867.

Of Cardinal Beaton's premises, he told his readers:

We observed that the roof of the turret was giving way, while the walls were also getting into a ruinous state, the proprietor being unwilling, it seems, to expend money on repairing the property as he expects the building to be cleared away in the course of a year or two.

The wine cellars of the palace are now used as dwelling-houses, and very dingy residences they are. It was in one of the transformed chapels, nearly half-way up the wynd, that the first cases of cholera in the parish broke out.

The rooms in this building are very badly constructed – the aim

The once-proud palace of Cardinal Beaton at the junction of Blackfriars' Wynd and the Cowgate was a prime example of a once-fashionable building falling through neglect and overcrowding into a revolting slum. The crusading zeal to improve the lot of those condemned to lives of abject poverty resulted in the Improvement Act of 1867, which saw virtually all of the dilapidated buildings demolished, and along with those clearances went part of the city's history.

of the proprietor having evidently been to make a large number of apartments without regard to the comfort of the tenants. What appears to have been one of the lobbies of the chapel has been partitioned off into small rooms, which are rented at 1s (5p) a week and upwards.

The family attacked by the cholera consisted of father, mother, and five children, of whom the mother and two children died. The father was a gardener in one of the nurseries, earning 12s a week; and the mother, in order to eke out a livelihood, occasionally went out selling fish. The house which this family of seven persons occupied is about 5 feet broad by about 12 feet long, the partition sheltering the apartment from the outer passage being very thin.

There is a large number of low, ill-ventilated, and ill-lighted dwellings in this wynd but in very many cases the buildings might be renovated with advantage, as the walls of not a few of the houses are very massive.

As the implications of the 1867 Act were enforced, Beaton's Palace building was finally demolished in 1874, together with most of the buildings in the wynd, which was then turned into the new Blackfriars Street.

SCOTTISH MINT

Not far away was the final Scottish Mint with its original entrance in Todrick's Wynd. The 'venerable quadrangle' of the mint, or Coinyie House, was in the Cowgate at the foot of the wynd, and the oldest part of what was to become over the years a large group of buildings had a 1574 date, although it was some years later before the mint finally moved in. These were partially castellated and designed to be defended if necessary against assault.

The first mint was in the outer court of Holyrood Palace, close to Horse Wynd, and then moved to the Castle for greater safety in 1559. It is likely that this building was demolished in the 1574 siege by English troops, and there was then a need for a new Coinyie or Cunzie House. There was also a mint briefly at the foot of Candlemaker Row, at its junction with the Grassmarket during the regency of Mary of Guise, the name sticking to the old house long after its money-making days were over.

The Cowgate mint featured a magnificent hall which was the scene of a banquet given to Danish nobles and ambassadors in 1590. The meal was 'at the requeist of the Kingis Majhestie, and for the honour of the toun', and James VI and his Queen Anne graced the occasion.

At one time, George Heriot, the goldsmith to the king, owned a large tenement on the north side of the mint court, and in his will he suggested it would be a suitable place for the hospital school he endowed. It was, however, found after his death to be in a ruinous state and unsuitable for 'Jinglin' Geordie's' proposed purpose. The new hospital was built at Lauriston, and his tenement was demolished to be replaced by another.

Goldsmiths connected with the mint seemed to live in some of the apartments in the courtyard, and that would probably explain how Heriot came to buy the northern tenement.

In its last days as a producer of coins – a right removed by the Treaty of Union in 1707 – the mint is described as having the coining house in the ground floor of the building on the north side of the courtyard. In the adjoining house in the east, the coins were polished and prepared for circulation.

At the Union, a ceremony to destroy the dies took place in the mint, and the properties went into other uses, including being used as homes by such eminent townsfolk as Lord Hailes and the distinguished medical man Lord Cullen. Most of the mint property was finally cleared in 1877, having reached the stage of 'no return' for decent housing.

Running out of the Cowgate southwards were two other familiar routes – the High School Wynd and Horse Wynd. The former was originally the access way granted to the Black Friars to their priory. When the High School came to be built in the former kirkyard of the monks, the association with the school was tagged to the old pathway. A new school replacing its 1578 forerunner was built in 1777, and has been successfully used as part of the Royal Infirmary and by the University of Edinburgh.

Horse Wynd followed the line of the lower part of Guthrie Street, the steps up to Chambers Street, and West College Street. It was one of the oldest approaches to the town, its name indicating that its width could cater for horse traffic.

The 19th century generally saw huge changes to Edinburgh as the city spread far from its original royalty and much of the medieval architecture was swept aside.

Square Deals

The Improvement Act of 1867 meant the end of two old squares which stood on the route of the new Chambers Street (1871–2) along the north side of the Old College of the University and the museum.

Argyle Square, which is shown in the 1742 map, was possibly the first of the squares with terraced houses, and the last vestiges went in 1871. It was occupied by distinguished citizens, and on its east side stood the Trades

OPPOSITE.
Pupils made their way to the old Royal High School in High School Yards to the south of the Cowgate along a narrow track beneath the windows of some attractive houses. The High School Wynd followed the original access to the Black Friars' priory, which was destroyed in the Reformation rioting in the town.

Maiden Hospital. Opposite the hospital was Minto House, the first town house of Lord Minto from the early 1700s. It was in time sub-divided, and in 1829 was fitted out as a surgical hospital. Among other buildings demolished to make way for the new street were the Gaelic Church and the Meeting House of Scottish Baptists.

Adam Square was close to South Bridge, and housed the School of Arts and Watt Institution until 1872, when the construction of Chambers Street saw the loss of another slice of the town.

The other open area in this part of town was Brown Square, which incorporated a group of houses called Society. They were built by the Society of Brewers in 1598.

The square itself was a small oblong, about 200 feet by 150 feet, and was developed by James Brown, who went on to construct George Square. He built Brown Square between 1763 and 1764, his fine mansions being declared 'an extremely elegant improvement'. The north and east sides were taken down for Chambers Street and the western part houses had gone when George IV

'That very elegant square, called Brown Square', as it was described in the Edinburgh Advertiser *in 1764, was an early example of a change in housing style in Edinburgh. Its builder, James Brown, went on to develop George Square in the 1760s, the first major residential scheme outside the Old Town. The last remains of Brown Square were demolished in the 1960s to provide a site for an extension to the Chambers Street museum, although the ground remained vacant for many years.*

Bridge was built between 1827 and 1836. The south side remained until the 1960s, when it was cleared to open the way for an extension to the Royal Scottish Museum.

Another South Side quarter was Alison Square, originally a large mass of building, according to Chambers, between Nicolson Street and the Potterrow. It was built in the middle of the 18th century. Marshall Street was driven through the centre of the great tenement in the 1870s.

CHARITY WORKHOUSE

The area round Bristo formerly contained a number of significant buildings, including the Charity Workhouse of 1743. Raised by voluntary contributions, it stood 70 yards or so south-west of the Bristo Port, and the poor inmates were originally allowed to keep two pence out of every shilling they earned.

The office of the ill-fated Darien enterprise was located nearby, a 1698

The Charity Workhouse provided much-needed shelter for men, women and children, and from its inception in 1743 was a prominent feature near the Bristo Port. It stood on what is now the site of the drill hall off Forrest Road and was originally supported by collections at church doors, charitable donations and citizens' contributions, together with a tax on rents.

two-storey and solid edifice, but till its demise was described as being a 'melancholy and desolate memorial to that unfortunate enterprise'.

Darien House – 'a substantial and somewhat handsome structure of ashlar-work in the French style' – was abandoned for commercial purposes and became the public lunatic asylum, populary known as the Bedlam, associated with the workhouse. A further house, known as the cells, was also part of the city Bedlam.

In 1842 and the following year, Forrest Road was formed through the workhouse grounds to the Middle Meadow Walk, and an old lodge which stood at the head of the walk and adjoining George Watson's Hospital grounds was removed by the Road Trustees.

The managers of the Charity Workhouse, conscious of the developing town and the pressure on its site, purchased the estate of Craiglockhart, south-west of Morningside, and built a poorhouse, which received its first inmates in 1870. The managers sold the old buildings and the grounds, which are now Teviot Place, Bristo Place and Forrest Road and Hill.

This house and the Darien building were removed in 1871 and the workhouse a few years later. The drill hall, just off Forrest Road, is pretty much the workhouse site. The Teviot Row buildings and site, having been purchased for the University Medical School, were removed in 1878.

The Craiglockhart poorhouse, where as many as 950 inmates were recorded by 1894, became Glenlockhart Old People's Home after the Second World War, and after further improvements in the 1960s became known as Greenlea. In 1987 it closed, and the main buildings were converted into housing and its grounds filled with modern flats.

Another workhouse was opened by the West Kirk (St Cuthbert's) parish in 1762 and that was finally cleared when the Caledonian Railway encroached on to the land at the foot of Lothian Road. A combined poorhouse of St Cuthbert's and the Canongate was built and that came to be the original heart of the hospital formed in 1927, now the Western General in Crewe Road.

One of the most telling observations on the state of old Edinburgh came from the historian and artist J. Bruce Home, who made a provisional list of old houses remaining in the High Street and Canongate.

It may safely be said that, since 1860, two-thirds of the ancient buildings in the Old Town of Edinburgh have been demolished.' While accepting that many had to be removed in the interests of hygiene, he felt that the 'more important examples' might have been retained and lifted into more conspicuous view.

Unfortunately, the actual process has been widely different. Destruction, widespread, ruthless, and indiscriminating, has been the rule; rarely has any consideration beyond the most baldly utilitarian been allowed to influence the decision, and the result is that a large proportion of our most valuable historic and architectural remains has been irretrievably lost to the city and to posterity.

he wrote for the first volume of the *Book of the Old Edinburgh Club*, published in 1908.

This process, which has gone on practically unchecked for over sixty years, has reached a point when, if aught of the venerable aspect and romantic interest of our city is to be maintained, an entirely different policy must be inaugurated. A united and vigorous effort must be made to rescue from the hands of the house-wrecking Philistine all that is possible of the few relics which still survive. Failing such effort the fatal 'too late' must be the epitaph of the famous Old Town of Edinburgh.

One of those he doubtless had in mind was ...

THE BOW HEAD

One of the most eye-catching sights in the town was the 'antique fabric' standing at the head of the West Bow at the corner of the Lawnmarket.

OPPOSITE.
The tenement land which stood at the stop of the West Bow where it sloped away from the Lawnmarket was long known as the Old Bowhead. Its demolition in 1878 'by the vandalistic action of the then existing civil authorities' was condemned by many, including the artist historian J. Bruce Home who recorded many of the city's old buildings before they joined the rubble piles. The caption on his sketch says simply: 'Old Bow Head destroyed 1878'. Thomas Nelson, the printer and publisher, had his premises here.

Old Bow Head

From humble beginnings in the Bow Head, the Thomas Nelson Parkside Works, backing onto Holyrood Park, were one of the biggest printing houses in a city which counted that trade as one of its specialities. Many printing and publishing firms flourished, but changes in technology brought a sad decline in the traditional trade.

Nelson's Parkside Works were closed and the building demolished. The Scottish Widows' office rose in its place in 1972.

'Reared ere Newton's law of gravitation was dreamt of,' says Wilson, and put up by builders who 'had discovered the art of constructing houses from the chimney-tops downward'.

> A range of slim wooden posts sustains a pile that at every successive storey shoots farther into the street, until it bears some resemblance to an inverted pyramid. It is a fine example of an old burgher building.

There was a piazza on the ground floor at the top of the Bow, with the beams of the upper floors projecting over it. With elevations onto the Lawnmarket and the West Bow, its occupants had a fine view of many of the ceremonial entries into the town in earlier days. Royal processions came through the West Port and into the Grassmarket before tackling the steep slope of the Bow to reach the Lawnmarket and continue down the High Street and through the Canongate to the Palace of Holyroodhouse.

The gables and eaves were richly carved and it was one of the last remaining reminders in the old town of an ancient timber land. Its age and attractiveness, however, could not ensure its future. It was demolished in 1878 – doubtless on the grounds that it was then in a ruinous condition and was not worth preserving.

Home, however, says the tenements of the Bow head 'were unnecessarily and unfortunately' demolished by civic authority – 'an irreparable loss to the antiquities of the city'.

Thomas Nelson, the publisher, had his first premises here and used an etching of the house as his company emblem.

Allan Ramsay's House

Another well-known house which was a feature of the High Street was still called Allan Ramsay's, long after the poet had moved first to the Luckenbooths and then to his much grander new home around which the Ramsay Garden complex was to be formed. Allan Ramsay's house stood at the head of Halkerston's Wynd and was timber-fronted 'at the sign of the Mercury, opposite Niddry's Wynd', with the traditional outside stone stairway to the upper level. It was demolished in 1899.

ABOVE AND OPPOSITE.

The poet Allan Ramsay had his shop and house in the High Street at the head of Halkerston's Wynd before he moved his publishing and bookselling business into the Luckenbooths beside St Giles'. He also built a fine new house, known as the 'Goose Pie', on the northern slopes of Castlehill. The house, extended by the poet's painter son, also Allan, became the nucleus of the Ramsay Garden complex developed by Patrick Geddes, the town planning pioneer.

CHAPTER 10

'DESECRATION'

Just how much the Old Town changed in the 19th century is indicated by the following.

Writing in 1890 for the introduction of the new edition of his *Memorials of Edinburgh* Sir Daniel Wilson looks back over the previous 50 years.

While the West Bow and the Castle Hill, Blackfriars' and St Mary's Wynds, Blyth's Close, St Ninian's Row, and many another vanished nook of picturesque aspect or historic interest, still remained ... the Palace of Mary of Guise; the haunted dwelling of Major Weir; the lodging of Bishop Bothwell, associated with one of the tenderest of old Scottish ballads ("Lady Ann Bothwell Vallow"); Robert Gourlay's historic mansion, alternately abode of nobles, foreign ambassadors, and other honoured guests, and place of durance of men of historic note throughout the sixteenth century; and that of Sir Thomas Hope, now less rich in some of the succeeding age; have all disappeared.

The beautiful Collegiate Church of Mary of Gueldres has given place to a railway station; and St Margaret's Well, with the legendary virtues of St Triduana's healing fountain has suffered a like fate ...

On the northern slope of the ridge along which the High Street

OPPOSITE.

Possibly the greatest architectural destruction in the 19th century was the removal of the medieval Trinity College Church to make way for an extension to the railway lines which had been allowed into the former valley of the Nor' Loch. The church, founded in 1460, and its associated Trinity Hospital lay below the steep crags of Calton Hill, and their removal was described by Lord Cockburn as a 'scandalous desecration'. Stones from the church were carefully numbered as the Gothic building was dismantled, with the intention of rebuilding on another site. Some of the numbered stones can still be seen in the former Trinity College Church apse, now the Brass Rubbing Centre, between the High Street and Jeffrey Street.

runs, Cockburn Street has displaced the old closes and wynds between the Cross and the Tron; and Jeffrey Street has still more effectually completed the work of destruction eastward to the Nether Bow. The great fire of 1824 left few traces of elder centuries on the southern slope of St Giles' and the Tron; but further eastward the destruction of Blackfriars' Wynd has effaced a thoroughfare only secondary in picturesque attractions and historic interest to the quaint old West Bow.' [Part of what is called Bishop Bothwell's house can still be seen off Advocate's Close.]

TRINITY COLLEGE CHURCH

Of all the acts of destruction perpetrated in Edinburgh in the 19th century, none equalled that of the removal of Trinity College Church and Hospital nestling in the valley below the Calton Hill and between Leith Wynd and the North Bridge. Its crime? It stood in the way of the railway, which was now allowed into the valley of the former Nor' Loch, and the station needed to be expanded.

The church was founded by Mary of Gueldres, consort of James II, in 1460 in memory of her husband. Dedicated to the Holy Trinity, the Blessed Virgin, St Ninian and All Saints, it was a magnificent medieval structure, built on the

The North British Railway Company wanted to expand the station beneath the North Bridge and the ground occupied by Trinity College Church and Hospital was the obvious target. Thus Edinburgh lost its magnificent medieval church.

site of a former St Ninian's Chapel.

On the church's south side stood the manse facing, on the other side of Leith Wynd, the Trinity Hospital, part of the Mary of Gueldres foundation. The hospital, which became ruinous, was moved in 1585 to the site of the manses, which were destoyed in 1558, at the time of the Reformation fervour in the town.

Trinity Church itself was not finished according to the wishes of its foundress, only the choir and transept being completed, and the nave was never built.

After the Reformation the church eventually passed into the ownership of the Town Council in 1567 and that meant that three centuries later they were in a position to sell the property to the North British Railway Company, who demolished it in 1848 for Waverley Station. Both the property used as the Trinity Hospital which 'provided a resting place for many generations of the genteel poor of the city', and the church were removed from this ancient site, but a condition of the church's demolition was that it would be rebuilt elsewhere.

The stones were therefore numbered and stored on Calton Hill while the search for a new location went on. Five sites were put forward – the corner of Calton Hill adjoining the steps in Regent Road; to the east of the Burns

Before the railway came into the drained valley of the Nor' Loch part of the ground below the North Bridge was used for the city's markets. The arrival of the railway into the city centre meant big changes had to be made.

Monument, also in Regent Road; East Princes Street Gardens at the south end of Waverley Bridge; Market Street; and the fifth at Ireland's woodyard in Leith Wynd.

A complicated series of legal wrangles took place between the Church and the anti-Church members of the Council over how much could be spent on a new church, among other matters. At the end of the day, in 1872, a new Holy Trinity Church was started on a site in Jeffrey Street. The stones of the old Trinity Church which had lain on the Calton Hill for 30 years were now much depleted, Edinburgh's citizens having helped themselves. What is now called the Trinity College Apse (or Brass Rubbing Centre), behind the north side of the High Street, is all that remains of Mary of Gueldres' church, and you can see the numbers on many of the stones used in the rebuilt section of the Jeffrey Street church, which itself was removed in the 20th century.

Mary of Gueldres was buried within 'the Queen's College', and Wilson bemoaned that her resting place was not marked with a stone after 'so irreverent and sacriligeous an act'.

Describing the church's demolition as a 'scandalous desecration', Cockburn said:

It was not only the oldest, but almost the only remaining Gothic structure in Edinburgh; and those who understood the subject, revered it as one of great architectural interest.

Yet this church was sacrificed, not to the necessities, but to the mere convenience of a railway. The railway had been finished, and was in action. But it wanted a few yards of more room for its station, and those it got by the destruction of the finest piece of old architecture in Edinburgh.

Cockburn was very much against the railway being allowed into the valley at all. In his polemic letter to Lord Provost William Ivory in 1849, 'On the Best Ways of Spoiling the Beauty of Edinburgh', the irate judge thunders:

> Those by whom, or for whom, the railways have been allowed to get into the Princes Street Gardens will, of course, justify, and affect to applaud, that permission and this even on reasons of taste. The rest of the world is very nearly unamimous in condemning it as a lamentable and irreparable blunder.
>
> It greatly dimishes the ornamental space; it disturbs and vulgarises what remains; it has introduced into ground by far the worthiest in the whole city of protection, parties who must always have a strong and restless interest hostile to all the interests of taste and recreation.

Close by the Trinity complex stood the Physic Garden, the precursor to the Royal Botanic Garden. The Physic Garden moved to a site on the west side of Leith Walk, where the new garden was laid out under the supervision of Professor John Hope, the King's Botanist, who died in 1786. The old garden was abandoned about 1770.

St Ninian's Row

The 1840s clearances for the new station also meant the end for a picturesque row of cottages and houses, St Ninian's Row, sometimes called 'the Beggar Row'. One of the stoutest buildings here was the hall of the Canongate Cordiners with a traditional carving, 'God Bliss the Cordiners of Edinburgh, wha built this house'. At one time, St Ninian's Row, on the line now of Low Calton, was a route from the end of Leith Wynd outside the Nether Bow to Leith Walk.

The hamlet of St Ninian's Row, nestling under the crags of the Calton Hill, was demolished as the railway expanded and other projects were planned at the eastern end of Princes Street.

ORPHAN HOSPITAL

The Orphan Hospital stood some 100 yards north of Trinity College Church and occupied part of the latter's burial ground. The hospital was conceived by a town merchant, Andrew Gardiner, in 1733, starting in a house, to provide shelter and education for poor and destitute children. Work on the hospital building, with its distinctive slender, pointed spire, started in June 1734, but it finally fell to the North British Railway Company in 1845, by which time a new orphanage had been built in open countryside close to Belford Road. Beside the main building, with its tower on which the clock from the demolished Nether Bow was placed, the Orphan Hospital had a small infirmary and a laundry.

The Orphan Hospital was another victim of the North British Railway Company's expansion in 1845 and the striking building joined the 'lost' list. The hospital nestled in the valley near Trinity College Church, close to where the General Post Office building was erected at the foot of North Bridge. A new orphanage was built at Belford, and that building is now the Dean Gallery.

Lady Glenorchy's Chapel, which stood in the low ground between the Orphan Hospital and the Trinity College Church, about 100 yards to the east of the northern arch of the North Bridge, was also removed as part of the rail expansion. The chapel was founded and endowed in 1772 by Wilhelmina Maxwell, who married John, Viscount Glenorchy. She feued part of the Orphan Hospital ground to erect a chapel at her own expense, replacing accommodation she had rented at St Mary's Chapel in Niddry Wynd. The chapel opened in 1774, and removed in 1844–5, eventually finding a new setting in Roxburgh Place on the South Side.

Leith Wynd itself, with its western edge the boundary for so many years of the Old Town, has now disappeared, although the west side of part of Jeffrey Street marks its line, but the remainder went in a further expansion of Waverley Station at the end of the 19th century. The old right of way was kept by a pedestrian bridge, now unused, over the station roof.

THEATRE ROYAL

The Theatre Royal, at the north-east end of North Bridge in Shakespeare Square, opened in 1769 'following the tide of fashionable emigration' to the New Town. It was built on the Orphan's Park, named after the Orphan Hospital. On or near the site in the 16th and 17th centuries stood Dingwall's Castle – a square tower with a round tower at each angle. Its name is attributed to Sir John Dingwall, who was Provost of Trinity College Church before the Reformation. Some fragments of the castle were reputedly found in the cellars of the Theatre Royal when it was demolished (in 1860).

The theatre superseded the old Canongate Concert Hall in Playhouse Close, opened in 1747 and closed in 1786. The battle to get theatre established in the town was a long and bitter one. Arnot gives an account of a group of travelling players who came to Edinburgh shortly after 1715. They were led by Signora Violante, 'an Italian lady, celebrated for feats of strength, postures, and tumbling, disgustful in any, but, in a woman, intolerable. At that period, however, people were not of this opinion.'

Standing in Shakespeare Square at the east end of Princes Street at its junction with North Bridge, the Theatre Royal was a very popular attraction from its opening night in 1769. The final performance came in May 1859 and the theatre, along with the remains of Shakespeare Square, made way for the GPO building which has subsequently been transformed behind its façade.

The 'virago' fitted up a house at the foot of Carrubber's Close for her shows, and later collected a company of English comedians for another visit to Edinburgh. For some years a strolling company of players visited, but they met with a great deal of opposition.

'The Presbyterian clergy were possessed with the most illiberal and violent animosity against the stage,' says Arnot. In 1727, backed by the ministers, the magistrates tried to expel the comedians from the town. They, however, went to the Court of Session to protest at the magistrates' action 'and continued to act notwithstanding the fulminations of the clergy'.

From then on, every two or three years, an itinerant company would come to the town, occasionally renting the Tailors' Hall in the Cowgate.

In 1737, an attempt by the poet and playwright Allan Ramsay to establish a theatre in Carrubber's Close was extinguished by the magistrates who succeeded in closing it down very quickly. The clergy also continued to battle on, but their protests simply seemed to boost the size of the audiences at the various shows when they came along.

In 1746, the foundation stone of a proper theatre was laid in the Canongate, west of St John's Street, and it was recognised as a proper playhouse, giving its name to the close. Technically it was operating outwith the law, but eventually a bill was presented to Parliament enabling the king to license a theatre in Edinburgh.

Thus a new theatre was started in 1768 in Shakespeare Square at the east end of Princes Street, opening to its first house in 1769. By 1786 the Canongate playhouse was closed.

The new theatre brought respectability to the stage in Edinburgh, even if its 'mean and barnlike appearance' might have been a bit off-putting. It had, however, a portico and on the point of its roof was a statue of William Shakespeare; on the sides were the comic and tragic muses.

The inside, however, was 'not wanting accommodations' and theatregoers gladly paid 3 shillings (15p) for the boxes and the pit; 2 shillings for the first gallery, and 1 shilling for the upper or second gallery. When the theatre raised its curtain, it faced the green slope at Multrees Hill, where Register House and St James' Square would be built.

OPPOSITE.
Tailors' Hall in the Cowgate was built in 1621, and extended in 1757 for the Incorporation of Tailors. It was viewed as the grandest of the guild halls. Among its many uses was that of a theatre, music hall and brewery. Until 1940 the premises were fronted by a very fine tenement bearing the tailors' crest over the entranceway to the courtyard behind. The hall stood unused for many years and was slowly decaying, but has now been restored as a restaurant and bar complex.

One of the greatest successes of all the plays and entertainments presented in the Theatre Royal was Walter Scott's operatic version of *Rob Roy*.

The Government, anxious to provide Edinburgh with a new General Post Office, bought the site, and the final performance was on 25 May 1859, including a farewell address from its manager, R.H. Wyndham.

Shakespeare Square – 'a semi-rectangle, alike mean in architecture and disreputable in character' – itself disappeared, partly with the opening up of the eastern end of Princes Street and the construction of Waterloo Place by Acts of 1813–14 and the adoption of Archibald Elliot's design in 1815 and then with the end of the theatre. The square had consisted of a straight row of buildings stretching from the top of Leith Street, ending on the south at the back of the Orphan Hospital.

On the sites of the theatre and the former Dingwall's ancient castle rose the GPO building, whose foundation stone was laid on 23 October 1861, by the Prince Consort, Prince Albert. On the same day he performed a similar duty at the museum site in what was to be Chambers Street.

CHAPTER 11

EXODUS

The first major exodus from the confined Old Town was to George Square, started in 1766, and then to the New Town, designed by James Craig, who laid in 1767 the foundation stone for the first houses in what is now Thistle Court (then Rose Court) between George Street and Thistle Street. The plan prepared by Craig, a young architect and draughtsman, was felt to be the most promising of those submitted in a competiton in 1766 to develop a new suburb on the land on the far side of the Nor' Loch, where there was open countryside, running up to a distinctive ridge from the water and then sloping sharply downwards to the north.

It was basically a pretty simple layout for three principal streets, with St Andrew and Charlotte Squares at the east and west end respectively. He did, however, propose a large circus at the crest of the hill where Frederick Street joined George Street, but the Town Council did not favour this suggestion and the streets were laid out in straight lines. Something of the envisaged scheme was lost there because Craig planned a church on the extremity of either square, setting off George Street.

Sir Lawrence Dundas beat the Town Council to it, by taking the feu in St Andrew Square of the ground where the church would have been placed and building a mansion house (now, much extended, the Royal Bank of Scotland building, set in its own grounds). That is why St Andrew's and St George's Church stands where it does, between St David Street and Hanover Street. The original great domed church in Charlotte Square, St George's, is now in secular use, as West Register House, one of the many former ecclesiastical buildings to have had a change of use.

Craig's New Town was followed by the Northern New Town, stretching down the hill almost to Canonmills, and then the Western New Town, based on the Melville Street axis. Its extremity is completed by the Victorian crescents of Grosvenor and Lansdowne and the others. Linking them were the old

Deanhaugh Estate, where the artist Sir Henry Raeburn created the gem of Ann Street and its surrounding streets, and the development of the Moray estate.

And there were also plans for an Eastern New Town, reaching from the Calton Hill down to Leith Links, a massive enterprise had it come off. But its vision was lost after it eventually got under way in 1820.

Regent Terrace, Royal Terrace (completed finally in 1860) and Carlton Terrace were the 'top layer' on the crest of the hill, but the dramatic planned layout of avenues and squares and gardens ground to a halt after Leopold Place, Elm Row, Windsor Street and part of Hillside Crescent were completed. When it was taken up again in the 1880s, it was much modified with Victorian tenements. Commercial and rail intrusion also restricted the development, so The Mall (today's Easter Road) and the other Georgian-style streets were lost.

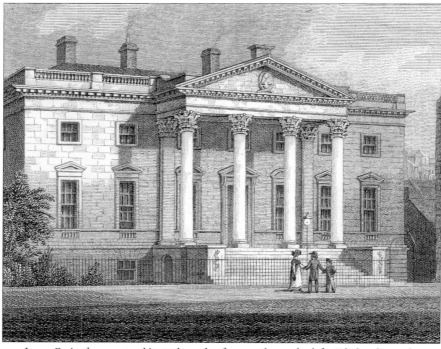

James Craig, the young architect whose plan for a northern suburb for Edinburgh won the competition of 1766, always felt he did not get the recognition he deserved for his work. But the New Town streets and squares have stood the test of time and were the foundation for subsequent extensions further north, east and west. The Physicians' Hall he designed was built in George Street in 1776, but the physicians appeared never to have been completely happy with it and sold the site to the Commercial Bank which ripped down Craig's building to erect a superb banking hall (now a restaurant and bar). The medical men bought a house in Queen Street and developed that into the present Royal College of Physicians of Scotland.

PHYSICIANS' HALL

Craig never felt he was properly recognised for the greatness of his New Town scheme, and he did not go on to get the architectural commissions he felt his work deserved.

He did, however, get the task of designing the Physicians' Hall in George Street. Its foundation stone was laid in 1776. The building, with an 84-foot long frontage, had a portico of four Corinthian columns and gave the College of Physicians a permanent home again after temporary refuge in the Royal Infirmary in Infirmary Street. Previously they had a hall in the garden at Fountain Close in the High Street.

But the physicians had money problems and were not entirely happy either with Craig's internal arrangements for the new building, which had a prominent position (opposite St Andrew's Church) in the central boulevard of his New Town.

A good offer came in from the Commercial Bank, which demolished the hall and in 1847 created the imposing building which in the late 20th century became a restaurant and bar complex.

The Royal College of Physicians built their new premises in Queen Street, which consisted of a single Georgian townhouse which was subsequently extended.

THE COUNTRYSIDE

As the New Town steadily expanded in the 19th century and swallowed up open countryside, much was inevitably lost. Villages, little farms, croft houses, rustic cottages, dairies – all were swept away as new houses and streets blossomed.

Lord Cockburn writes of the Earl of Moray's ground to the north of Charlotte Square being broken up in the 1820s for building:

> It was then an open field of as green turf as Scotland could boast of, with a few respectable trees on the flat, and thickly wooded on the bank along the Water of Leith. Moray Place and Ainslie Place stand there now. It was the beginning of a sad change, as we then felt. That well-kept and almost evergreen field was the most beautiful piece of ground in immediate connection with the town, and led the eye agreeably over to our distant northern scenery. How glorious the prospect, on a summer evening, from Queen Street!

We had got into the habit of believing that the mere charm of the ground to us would keep it sacred, and were inclined to cling to our conviction even after we saw the foundations digging. We then thought with despair of our lost verdure, our banished peacefulness, our gorgeous sunsets. But it was unavoidable. We would never have got beyond the North Loch, if these feelings had been conclusive. But how can I forget the glory of that scene! on the still nights on which ... I have stood in Queen Street, or in the opening at the north-west corner of Charlotte Square, and listened to the ceaseless rural corn-craiks, nestling happily in the dewy grass. It would be some consolation if the buildings were worthy of the situation; but the northern houses are turned the wrong way, and everything is sacrificed to the multiplication of feuing feet.

His Lordship was also concered about the increasing desecration – 'our lamentable error' – of trees around the town.

We massacre every town tree that comes in a mason's way; never sacrificing mortar to foliage,' he protested. 'I do not know a single instance in which the square and the line have been compelled to accommodate themselves to stems and branches. To a considerable extent this is a consequence of our climate, which needs sun and not shade. But there are many situations, especially in a town, where shade is grateful, and many where, without interfering with comfort, foliage, besides its natural beauty, combines well with buildings. And there was no Scotch city more strikingly graced by individual trees and by groups of them than Edinburgh, since I knew it, used to be.

How well the ridge of the old town was set off by a bank of elms that ran along the front of James' Court, and stretched eastward over the ground now partly occupied by the Bank of Scotland. Some very respectable trees might have been spared to grace the Espicopal Chapel of St Paul in York Place. There was only one large tree near its east end which was so well placed that some people conjectured it was on its account that the Chapel was set down there. I was at a consultation in John Clerk's house, hard by, when that tree was cut. On hearing that it was actually down we ran out, and well did John curse the Huns.

The old aristocratic gardens of the Canongate were crowded with trees, and with good ones. There were several on the Calton

Hill: seven, not ill grown, on its very summit. And all Leith Walk and Lauriston, including the ground round Heriot's Hospital, was fully set with wood. A group was felled about the year 1826 which stood to the west of St John's Chapel on the opposite side of the Lothian Road, and formed a beautiful termination of all the streets which join near that point.

One half of the trees, at the least, might have been spared, not only without injuring, but with the effect of greatly adorning, the buildings for which they have been sacrificed. Moray Place, in the same way, might have been richly decorated with old and respectable trees. But they were all murdered on the usual pretence of adjusting levels and removing obstructions.

It was with the greatest difficulty that Sir Patrick Walker, the superior of the ground, succeeded in rescuing the row in front of Coates Crescent from the unhallowed axes of the very vassals. It cost him years of what was called obstinacy.

I tried to save a very picturesque group, some of which waved over the wall at the west end of the jail on the Calton Hill. I succeeded with two trees: but in about four years they also disappeared. It only required a very little consideration and arrangement to have left the whole of these trees and many others standing without abating a single building.

But the sad truth is that the extinction of foliage, and the unbroken display of their bright free-stone, is of itself a first object with both our masons and their employers.

... AND THE VILLAGES

BROUGHTON

The villages which had once nestled in quiet seclusion felt the effects of the New Town. The most interesting was the baronial burgh of Broughton, which can be traced in name back to the 1128 charter of David 1 founding Holyrood Abbey. The village was to the north of the present Albany Street and was bounded by that road and what are now Broughton Place and Street, Barony Street and Old Broughton. The houses were mainly two storeys high with outside stairs and crowstepped gables. The original thatched roofs were replaced with tiles and each dwelling had a small area of ground with it.

Broughton Village was one of the communities swallowed up by the expanding New Town. At one time it was overseen by a baron baillie appointed by the Town Council and operated within its own framework of often harsh laws. Barony Street covers most of the village site today.

The village centre stood on the line of Barony Street and the village had its own tolbooth, with the date 1582 over its north door. It was removed in 1829, marking the end of the barony which was granted by James VI in 1569 to Adam Bothwell, Bishop of Orkney. The land eventually passed in 1636 to the Governors of Heriot's Hospital, who appointed a bailiff with the power of 'pit and gallows' – life and death – over its inhabitants.

In 1753, the tolbooth was let by the Governors as a store, although they retained the right to a meeting room there. It was another two-storey building with small grated windows and stairs leading to the central doorway. On either side of this entrance were stocks in which minor offenders were punished.

The development of the surrounding streets saw it removed, together with the gradual vanishing of the village houses. Broughton Market was built between Barony Street and Dublin Street in the 1840s, but only a remnant of the entrance gateway remains.

BELLEVUE LODGE

To the north of Broughton village, a road led to Canonmills by way of Bellevue and continued to Newhaven, while another ran westwards along the banks of

The Barony of Broughton boasted its own tolbooth where prisoners could be held, and meetings take place. The baron baillies had powers of 'pit and gallows' – the power to drown women in a pit and to hang men on a gibbet.

the Water of Leith. Two fine houses, of which there is now no trace, stood close to the village in what is now Drummond Place Gardens. George Drummond, six times holder of the post of Lord Provost and the visionary of the New Town, spent his latter years (1757–66) in a country house here. He had feued seven acres of land from the Governors of Heriot's Hospital and built Drummond Lodge. The comfortable and welcoming house was approached by a tree-lined avenue (now London Street) off the road to Canonmills.

'No part of the home scenery of Edinburgh was more beautiful than Bellevue,' says Cockburn. 'It seemed to consist of nearly all the land between York Place and Canonmills – a space now almost covered by streets and houses.'

Drummond died at the age of 79 in 1766, the year before the foundation stone of the first New Town houses was laid. His name, however, lives on in Drummond Place.

On the site of Drummond Lodge was built a large three-storey mansion called Bellevue. It was for General John Scott of Balcomie, a notorious gambler, and it is said the house came about as the result of a successful wager he made with the eminent citizen Sir Lawrence Dundas. In a card game with Scott, Dundas had foolishly pledged his own house on the east side of St Andrew Square and lost. However, the matter was resolved amicably when Dundas

Bellevue House or Lodge stood in what is now Drummond Place Gardens. It was built on the site of the house occupied by Lord Provost George Drummond. After his, death General John Scott occupied the new house, which was later bought by the government to serve as the Excise Office. It was demolished in 1844.

offered to build a new house for the military man, and General Scott appeared satisfied with the deal. The mansion of Bellevue was later acquired by the government and became the Excise Office before being demolished in 1844, when the Edinburgh, Perth and Dundee Railway Company built the tunnel running from Waverley Station to Scotland Street, undermining the property.

CANONMILLS

To the north, on the banks of the Water of Leith, and also within the Broughton barony's bounds, was the village of Canonmills, named after the monks of Holyrood who built mills on the lands of Broughton granted by David I. Over the centuries it grew in importance as a milling centre for the town, and close by in the hollow now overlooked by Royal Crescent on one side and Eyre Crescent on the other, lay the waters of Canonmills Loch. The last of it was still visible as a pond on a map of 1893.

When the loch was drained earlier, part of its site became the home of the Royal Patent Gymnasium, a place which drew thousands of curious townsfolk and other visitors. It opened in April 1865, and among the attractions were a

Water from the mill lades which served Stockbridge and Silvermills came into Canonmills Loch before finding its way back into the Water of Leith. The loch was used by a curling club and was a popular destination for people taking a stroll into the Canonmills countryside. Part of the loch's site is covered by Eyre Crescent and adjoining streets.

'rotary boat' with seating for 600 rowers, a giant see-saw and a 'velocipede paddle merry-go-round' became 160 feet in circumference, with seating for another 600. Another part of the site Scotland Street railway station.

PICARDIE

Two other villages effectively vanished under the New Town. One was called Picardie, which went with the extension of York Place into Picardy Place. The village ground was sold by Heriot's Governors around 1730 to the town to provide a place of refuge for silk weavers driven from France after the edict of Nantes. They named the village Picardie after their native province. In 1800 the area of the village was feued for housing and the little cottages disappeared.

There is an interesting sidelight on the endeavours of the weaving folk. They tried to establish a silk manufactory and laid out a large plantation of mulberry trees on the slopes of Multrees Hill (roughly where the St James' Centre now stands). It is said that the vagaries of the Scottish climate, however, put an end to their growing ambitions and many of the immigrants almost certainly turned their talents from silk to linen weaving.

A refuge for silk weavers driven from France, the village of Picardie was lost when York Place was extended into Picardy Place and the land feud for housing at the start of the 19th century.

SILVERMILLS

In the dip behind St Stephen's Church at the foot of St Vincent Street lay the village of Silvermills, which still gives its name to the area. A few traces of old mills and other buildings can be found, but it is now primarily a modern housing and commercial area. Originally it sat close to the Water of Leith within the ancient Barony of Broughton and near to another village, Stockbridge, now a thriving New Town enclave.

Chambers suggests its name came about in the early 17th century, when abundant supplies of silver were found in old Linlithgowshire (now West Lothian). Barrels of ore were sent to the mint in London and found to give a good yield of the precious metal. It was thought more businesslike to mill the ore on the Water of Leith much closer to Edinburgh, however, and a milling operation was set up.

King James VI and I heard of the enterprise and felt, according to Chambers, that such a productive enterprise should benefit the public, and presumably himself. Accordingly, he bought the mine, which had been named 'God's blessing' by its owner, but, to royal dismay, it did not produce the amounts of silver he had anticipated. James withdrew, having burned his fingers in his speculation.

Part of the abandoned plant, Chambers surmised, was based in Silvermills, and hence the name.

Dean House and Villages

Dean House was demolished in 1845 so that its grounds and the little hamlet of Dean there could be converted into the Dean Cemetery. A 'fine old aristocratic dwelling', it was the house of the Nisbets of Dean and was inscribed with dates, the earliest 1614, and armorial bearings. Some of the stones were incorporated into the walls of the Dean Cemetery. The house's departure also heralded the gradual demise of the hamlet of Dean, which stood close to the house and was a distinct grouping of cottages.

The community beside the Water of Leith now called the Dean Village was for centuries known as the Water of Leith Village. It has changed out of all recognition. No longer do mills hum by the waterside; no longer does the skinnery and tannery float its stench across the valley; no longer does the playground ring with the cries of school children; and the last shop is gone. Old mills and the Baxters' (bakers') granary of 1675 are now homes, and the whole village is now residential, with many new properties built in the past few years, including on the site of the old skinnery.

Upstream a little stood Sunbury House, and its last remnants, together with the distillery there, vanished shortly after the Second World War.

Piershill Barracks

Also built very much in the countryside, the cavalry barracks were on the eastern side of the town, close to the hamlet of Jock's Lodge, where there was a toll to collect payment from travellers. In the middle of the 18th century, a Colonel Piers, who commanded a corps of horse, occupied what became known as Piershill House, a large villa with ample stabling, on high ground to the north of the road at Jock's Lodge and overlooking Restalrig Village.

The house occupied the land that was to become the site of the officers' quarters of the barracks, built in 1793 for two regiments of cavalry. Piershill Barracks formed three sides of a quadrangle, a wall with gateways running along the line of the turnpike road. It was a place which attracted sightseers. As one observer commented:

> A stroll from the beautiful city to Piershill when the musical bands of the barracks are striving to drown the soft and carolling melodies of the little songsters on the hedges and trees of the subsession of Arthur's Seat, and when the blue Firth, with its many-tinted canopy

of clouds, and its picturesque display of islets and steamers, and little sailing boats on its waters, vies with the luxuriant lands upon its shore to win the award due to beauty, is indescribably delightful.

After a survey of conditions in the barracks was made in 1909, they were deemed unfit for cavalrymen and their animals. There was such a public outcry when the decision was announced at the prospect of losing the Royal Scots Greys, then based at Piershill, that eventually new cavalry barracks were built at Redford at Colinton.

Piershill continued in military use until 1934, and the site was then bought by the Council. The stone from the demolished barracks was used to build the working-class houses, as they were then described, that form the East and West Piershill Squares round open ground.

CHAPTER 12

MARKET DAYS

From the milling and farming communities round the town came much of the produce which filled the many markets of the Old Town.

At one time, the High Street resounded with the cries of market traders pushing their wares, and it has been noted how the king stepped in to allocate specific areas for the sale of certain goods. Changing conditions in the town, however, meant that the various markets moved round subsequently.

An Act of Council of 1840 set out the boundaries of the ten markets which were then operating. They were: meal, corn and grain in the Grassmarket in the corn exchange building; sheep, lamb and pig markets between Fountainbridge and Cowfeeder Row (now High Riggs); a cattle market in the Grassmarket, West Port and King's Stables Road; a horse market in the Grassmarket; a straw market in the Grassmarket; a fish market and meat market between North Bridge and Fleshmarket Close; a wholesale and retail vegetable market under North Bridge and between it and the old Physic Garden; a wholesale fruit market adjoining the vegetable market; a fish market in part of the vegetable market; and a poultry market between North Bridge and Fleshmarket Close.

An old market, mainly for ewes, was held at House o' Muir on the slopes of the Pentlands. This ended in 1870 when the 'great ewe sale' was transferred first to the Meadows and then to Lauriston Place.

By 1874, when the Edinburgh Markets and Customs Act was passed, there were still eight separate markets in the town, but most of those closed due to the growth of shops and other retail outlets.

The fish market was held on ground now covered by part of the Waverley Station, and then at one of the arches in Cranston Street. It was superseded by the Newhaven fish market. Previously, the fish market was at the foot of Old Fishmarket Close – 'a steep, narrow, stinking ravine', says Cockburn.

The fish were generally thrown out on the street at the head of the close, whence they were dragged down by dirty boys or dirtier women; and then sold unwashed – for there was not a drop of water in the place – from old, rickety, scaly, wooden tables, exposed to all the rain, dust and filth; an abomination the recollection of which greatly impaired the pleasantness of the fish at a later hour of the day.

The flesh market was sited in Fleshmarket Close on ground eventually covered by *The Scotsman* building, and the retail poultry market was also held in that close.

The wholesale poultry, egg, butter and cheese market was held round the Tron Kirk, and again Cockburn has left us with a memory of the vegetable market stalls.

They were entirely in the hands of a college of old gin-drinking women, who congregated with stools and tables round the Tron Church. A few of the aristocracy of these ladies – the burgo-mistresses, who had established a superior business – the heads of old booths – marked their dignity by an awning of dirty canvas or tattered carpet; and every table had its tallow candle and paper lantern at night.

There was no water here either, except what flowed down the gutter, which, however, was plentifully used. Fruit had a place on the table, but kitchen vegetables lay bruised on the ground.

The Green Market, as the fruit and vegetable market was called, was moved under North Bridge and then enclosed. Its main access was along Canal Street, approximately the line of the northern carriageway into Waverley Station.

With the expansion of the railway and the amalgamation of the companies using Waverley Station, the North British Railway Company wanted to buy the land used by the fruit and vegetable markets. Eventually, after protracted negotiations, it was agreed that the Waverley Market should be built south of

OPPOSITE.
The name Fleshmarket Close – the close from the High Street which led to the meat market originally on the banks of the Nor' Loch – is self-explanatory. Today it runs across (Lord) Cockburn Street and down the side of The Scotsman Hotel to Market Street. The Old Fishmarket Close still runs southwards to the Cowgate as a reminder of where the fruits of the sea were once sold.

Princes Street beside a widened Waverley Bridge, and it was passed to the town in 1869, originally as an open site which was roofed in 1874. It was primarily used for fruit, vegetables and flowers. Later, when those traders moved to warehouses in Market Street – the Green Market is now at Sighthill – the Waverley Market was used for many purposes, including fairs, circuses, menageries, commercial exhibitions, Edinburgh Festival Fringe shows and public meetings. The site is now occupied by the Princes Mall shopping centre.

The corn and cattle markets also moved round the town. The meal market was shifted from the High Street by a Town Council instruction in 1540, and after several moves a new corn exchange and meal market building opened in the Grassmarket in 1849.

The Grassmarket itself was a bustle of markets in its time, and after the Council bought land at Lauriston Place, the cattle and sheep market moved there in 1844. When the Central Fire Station was put up in 1900 on an adjoining site, there was an inevitable clash between drovers and their animals and the horse-drawn fire engines trying to answer the call to a blaze. The sheep moved temporarily back to the Grassmarket, and in 1911 the cattle, horse and sheep sales were moved out to purpose-built premises at Gorgie, where a new corn exchange was also built.

A slaughterhouse was also situated beneath North Bridge, causing many complaints from pedestrians above about the smells and also the noise as animals were butchered. Originally, the slaughtermen had set up their 'shambles' on the southern bank of the Nor' Loch.

An enclosed building was formed as a result of the protests, but again rail expansion resulted in its demolition.

With no official slaughterhouse, booths for the trade sprung up, possibly as many as 75, and the Council was forced to take steps to remedy this unacceptable situation. A slaughterhouse was built in 1850 at Lochrin, near Tollcross, in an area which was being developed for tenement housing and led to a long battle by the Medical Officer of Health, Henry Littlejohn, to have it removed on grounds of public safety.

In 1911 it was taken out to Gorgie, beside the other markets. Now no slaughtering is carried out in Edinburgh. The last slaughterhouse site is occupied by a new ASDA superstore, the cattle market is a sports and leisure centre, the Corn Exchange hosts pop concerts. Another old 'dead meat' market building at the corner of Semple Street in Fountainbridge became a night-club venue.

There were at least three other market-places in what were then city suburbs. The Broughton Market, at the end of Barony Street, served much of the northern New Town, while the Stockbridge Market, opened in 1826, continued into the 20th century. You can still see the 'Butcher meat, fruit, fish and poultry' inscription over the archway in St Stephen Place. The Southern Market was in West Nicolson Street.

CHAPTER 13
'NOTHING REMAINS'

In the first decade of the 20th century those anxious to see old Edinburgh preserved were fighting a losing battle.

True, Advocate's Close still contained at its head some 'very ancient' houses, offsetting the damage to the lower part, which was demolished in 1884. But the 1580 house at the top of Warriston Close, still with some remains of its arcaded front, was removed in 1908, while next door the tenement frontage of Writers' Court went the same way when extensions were made to the City Chambers.

Two old houses in Stamp Office Close were designated slums and demolished in 1902. The house on the west side of the close was formerly the town house of the Earl of Eglintoun and his wife, Susannah, a great beauty. It later became Fortune's Tavern. What are described as 'quaint old houses' in Morrison's and Bailie Fyfe's Close were 'doomed' in 1902, and in the same year one of the last timber-fronted houses on the north side of the High Street and a fine stone mansion also went.

So often the writer, as he looks at the individual closes, comments sadly that 'nothing remains' of former times. And so we have to accept that the 1890s and early 1900s saw the erosion of much of the picturesque property which so entranced the caring citizen and visitor alike.

There was no longer a deep desire to live in the heart of the city, apart perhaps from the poorer residents, who had little option.

The attractiveness of the new houses and greenery of George Square, almost in the open countryside when it was started, and the spaciousness of the

OPPOSITE.
As the villas spread across the countryside of Merchiston, the old tower house of the Napier family stood firm in its grounds. There is an authentic reference to it in 1495. Now Merchiston Castle is a central feature of the Napier University campus at the eastern end of Colinton Road.

New Town streets with their stately houses, meant that the Edinburgh which had existed until the middle of the 18th century was undergoing a dramatic change.

While the New Town in its various stages developed on a line north of Princes Street, there followed the march of the detached villas and a new style of tenement building, reminiscent in some ways of the Old Town lands, but providing a better standard of living. The working-class quarters were created round the industrial growth in areas such as Fountainbridge, Dalry and Gorgie, while the ranges of streets in Marchmont and Bruntsfield and Comely Bank, for instance, were aimed more at the city's middle class.

As the villas sprang up round Mayfield, Grange, Church Hill, Merchiston, Morningside or Trinity, they came under fire from at least one trenchant critic, writer and Edinburgh son Robert Louis Stevenson.

'Day by day, one new villa, one new object of offence, is added to another,' he wrote.

All round Newington and Morningside, the dismallest structures keep springing up like mushrooms; the pleasant hills are loaded with them, each impudently squatted in its garden, each roofed and carrying a chimney like a house. And yet a glance of an eye discovers their true character. They are not houses: for they were not designed with a view to human habitation, and the internal arrangements are, as they tell me, fantastically unsuited to the needs of man. They are not buildings; for you can scarcely say a thing is built where every measurement is in clamant disproportion with its neighbour. They belong to no style of art, only to form a business much to be regretted.

The 'insufferably ugly' villa threatened the amenity of the town – 'and as this eruption keeps spreading on our borders, we have even further to walk among unpleasant sights, before we gain the front of air.'

It was possibly that loss of open land he had known as a boy more than anything which also helped to stiffen his outburst.

As the city ranged outwards, the march of new streets and housing estates approached and overswept many of the old villages, once self-sufficient communities in the countryside. Places such as Corstorphine, Slateford, Blackhall, Davidson's Mains, Liberton and Juniper Green were all swallowed up. Slateford Village, especially, is all but destroyed by road widening, and there is little trace of the milling and other industries on which it once relied.

Gilmerton, on the other hand, is still a recognisable village, at one time a

Once the biggest of all the mills on the banks of Edinburgh's river, the Water of Leith, the Kinleith Mill at Currie, has passed into history. On the river's banks stood many water-powered mills producing throughout the centuries a wide range of products. A survey in 1792 recorded 76 water-driven mills – 24 flour, 14 oatmeal, 12 barley, 7 saw, 6 snuff, 5 cloth fulling, 4 paper, 2 lint and 2 leather. Great complexes like McNabs., which started off as a bleach field and closed as a laundry, are gone from Slateford, and the biggest of the papermakers – Galloway's at Balerno and the Kinleith Mill – are no longer in business. McNab's site houses a cash-and-carry and will have a new food store, the Balerno site is smothered in housing, and at Kinleith the land still lies empty. Inglis Mill beneath the city bypass at Juniper Green vanished in 2004 to make way for more housing.

mining and limestone quarrying centre. The last coal pit closed in 1961.

'Gilmerton was long characterised simply as a village of colliers of a peculiarly degraded and brutal nature, as ferocious and unprincipled as a gang of desperadoes,' says James Grant in his *Old and New Edinburgh*.

By the early 1960s, Cramond Village had been renovated and the attractive cottages were quickly snapped up by residents wanting to live by the city's waterside. Another rural village, Swanston, nestling on the slopes of the Pentland Hills, was also restored by the Council. Redolent of Stevenson, whose family holidayed in a large house beside the village, the thatched roofs and white-washed walls of its little cottages, sitting above the city bypass, are now unique in the city.

Later extensions of the boundaries brought Balerno and Currie into the city, and the once huge pulsating paper-making plants of Galloway's and Kinleith Mills have disappeared.

Although an element of the once-rural life can still be seen around old churches or in the last of the cottages in the old villages, the general loss is immediately apparent. New building, particularly the sprawl of 'bungalow land' starting in the 1920s, saw farmland round the village communities vanish, and then came the large Council housing estates in places such as Craigmillar and Niddrie, Prestonfield, Restalrig, Lochend and Craigentinny.

The inexorable march of change was inevitably to cause major lossses to Edinburgh through the 20th century.

CHAPTER 14
BATTLE JOINED

PRINCES STREET

Princes Street was not designed by James Craig in his New Town plans of 1766 to be the principal street. It had an open vista, certainly, and he wanted the remnants of the Nor' Loch to be turned into an ornamental canal below street level with flourishing pleasure gardens.

Instead, George Street, the broad boulevard on the crest of the hill with a spacious square at either end, was to be the axis, with Queen Street to the north and Princes Street to the south the subsidiary roadways.

He, and the Town Council, saw this northern suburb, too, as a purely residential area, free from commerce. It was to be an elegant option to the congested, dirty, busy High Street and Lawnmarket. It was to bring a new look and a burst of fresh enthusiasm to a town in the doldrums, and it certainly succeeded on both scores.

But the Princes Street of fairly plain, stone-built, three-storey houses which slowly spread from east to west, was relatively quickly lost as its commercial potential was realised. Shops were opened in the ground floors or in the basements of the houses, and as business boomed so the front-room shop would extend to the back rooms as well, then upstairs. Then a house would be demolished, or at least the front of it, and it was turned over completely to business. Hotels followed, then bigger businesses, such as insurance companies, which tore down the original houses to build often in a magnificent style. Much later, the national high street superstore ventured in – Littlewoods first of all.

In no thoroughfare in Edinburgh, even in the Royal Mile, has so much happened so quickly. What was lost first of all was the view for the most easterly houses, because an enterprising developer, coachbuilder John Home, after some complicated negotiations with the Council, feued the land on the north-west corner of North Bridge, and gradually a collections of buildings was formed between St Ann's Street, which ran steeply (in a gradient of one in six) down the side of the bridge, and Canal Street, roughly on a line from the present Waverley Bridge to the North Bridge itself. The canal was shown as an ornamental stretch of water in Craig's New Town plan, reflecting his desire to incorporate a reflection of the Nor' Loch. It never happened.

In all, Home acquired a 162-foot-long frontage on the south side of Princes Street – from the bridge to the present Waverley Steps. An upholstery firm then feued more land to the west for workshops, but the Council agreed to the latter only on condition that the buildings did not rise above the level of Princes Street.

Not unnaturally, the street's residents were becoming concerned at what they saw as a breach of the New Town planned layout, and after legal action it was ruled that the workshops could go ahead below the level of Princes Street, but all the ground from there to Hanover Street should be 'kept and preserved in perpetuity as pleasure ground'. Technically, that might have permitted housebuilding on the south side of Princes Street from the foot of the Mound to the West End, but in 1816 an Act of Parliament prevented any such construction for all time.

Canal Street itself, with its houses facing across to the shambles and the fruit and vegetable markets, vanished with the redevelopment of Waverley Station in 1868, and the corner block at the foot of North Bridge was finally demolished in 1896, much of the property having been used as hotels.

The St Ann's Street tenements, however, went earlier, as did the street itself, and no one seemed to miss them.

The whole were reared and finished in the meanest and most irregular manner, presenting to the view over the parapet wall of the North Bridge a range of dirty and deformed chimmey tops and of heavy roofs, in which the most curious eye could scarcely discover any feature of the sublime or beautiful. They were occupied, too, exclusively, by keepers of ale-houses and small shops, or by chairmen, porters, and common mechanics; and, in particular, by a numerous and exalted colony of operative tailors, whose gay and flaring signboards were the first objects that struck the traveller as he crossed to the Old Town; and whose newly washed or dyed old clothes, of all odious colours and smells, were displayed from the upper stories of these tenements, none of which had either offices, or back court, or yard of any description.

An elegant Princes Street still showing signs of its original purely residential nature. James Craig's plan for the first New Town did not allow for commercial premises in the main streets, but very quickly the shopping potential of Princes Street in particular was realised, with businesses being opened in the ground floor and basement areas of the houses.

The Council reached an agreement with the owners of the St Ann's Street houses and the properties were demolished. New buildings, which in themselves raised an outcry, were put up and at the same time the North Bridge was widened. The objectors' concern was that the view from the Calton Hill westwards over the bridge would be affected.

On the site originally held by Home, the Balmoral Hotel, or still in the minds of older Edinburghers, the NB (North British), now stands. It was designed by W. Hamilton Beattie in a competition in 1895 and completed in 1902 for the rail company.

The fast-changing nature of Princes Street can be gauged from the Post Office Annual Directory of 1833, which lists the occupiers and occupations. From Nos 1 to 99, with only one or two exceptions, the properties had a commercial use – coach office, hotel, spirit merchant, saddler, bootmaker, dentist, tailor, straw-plait shop, staymakers, druggist, hairdresser, silk mercer, toy shop, watchmaker, bird stuffer, dealer in curiosities, booksellers, grocer, and so on – the whole gamut of suppliers for the town. The last house listed, No. 148, at the west end, contained a grocer and a coal merchant. The idea of a purely residential street was lost for ever.

It is hard to imagine that Jenners' store, the shopping queen of the street, was originally launched in 1838 in a small house at the corner of South St David Street by Charles Kennington and his partner, Charles Jenner, the business then being Kennington and Jenner. After Kennington's death, Jenner expanded the store by adjoining converted houses, but in 1892 his shop was destroyed by fire. From the ashes rose what has been described as a 'wondrous Renaissance compilation in pink stone' which was subsequently expanded.

The distinctive character of the 19th-century Princes Street has also been lost, as John Ruskin's description shows:

Princes Street is the grand promenade of the gay and fashionable, the resort of young and old, and of all who have nothing to do but to see and be seen. Here are the fair ones of the Scottish metropolis, elegantly attired, the roses on their cheeks glowing with a deeper and lovelier tint from exposure to this bracing atmosphere. Here young fellows swagger along, with or without cigars, sporting moustaches, whiskers, and imperials, in every variety of shape and in every stage of development.

Occasionally a military officer in his regimentals, a dashing sergeant, or a brace of rank and file in Highland costume, more rarely the fez of a Turk, lends variety to the scene, while now and then the white cravat of some professional relieves the monotony of the black stock.

Shops are here of every kind, displaying at their stately plate-glass windows, in forms the most alluring, all sorts of goods, wares, and merchandise – drapers, goldsmiths, printsellers, and bazaarists, vying with each other in the beauty, the splendour and attractiveness of the articles exhibited for sale; dentists and photographists, not less eager to catch the public eye, displaying in glass cases their choicest specimens of their professional skills. But, beside the great saloons on a level with the pavement, or approached by a flight of steps, the sunk areas teem with small shops, where are vended a thousand useful and ornamental articles and nick-knacks from a pin or baby's dress or a cap for mamma; from a caoutchouc (rubber) overcoat or air-cushion to a pair of gutta-percha foot preservers; from a supple-jack, or a wax doll to miniature Laocoon, Venus or Apollo.

But the attractiveness of Princes Street is not due alone to the shops, not to its hotels or public offices, or splendid New Club-house. Its popularity, if I may so express it, as a promenade arises from a combination of cases. Extending for nearly a mile from Register

House on the east, to the beautiful Episcopal chapel of St John's and Hope Street, on the west, and almost on a dead level throughout, which is no small recommendation in a city so remarkable for the steepness of its streets; its spacious pavement; its fine southern exposure; and forming, as it does, the great connecting link, by means of the North Bridge and the Mound, with the Old Town, it should seem as if it had been expressly designed to be, what it is, the leading thoroughfare and rendezvous of Edinburgh.

The 1949 Patrick Abercrombie and Derek Plumstead Civic Survey had proposed a gradual move towards a new-look Princes Street, to an overall pattern of blocks to replace the mish-mash of architectural styles which had developed over almost two centuries. A general acceptance of rebuilding led to the formation in 1954 of the Princes Street Panel to regulate redevelopment, and one of its introductions was a first-floor-level balcony along new frontages, the idea being to have a continuous walkway the entire length of the street. How the walkway would cross the streets joining Princes Street was never really resolved, and the scheme was abandoned at the end of the 1970s. The parts of the walkway which were constructed are there for all to see – the paths to nowhere.

Original houses can still be easily traced in Princes Street with ground-floor shop fronts, while other houses have been incorporated completely behind new frontages. The Victorian splendour is still there in the Jenners building (1893–5) and the Waverley Hotel (1883).

But crunch time came for the street in the second half of last century, when it was seen as ripe for redevelopment. Splendid Victorian edifices such as the Life Association and the New Club, between Hanover Street and Frederick Street, and the North British and Mercantile to the east became vulnerable to the developer. The old Balmoral Restaurant was rebuilt to provide a new store for Littlewoods, which has now left the street, and other new store frontages appeared.

The decision to demolish the North British and Mercantile office to make way for a large chain store sparked off a furious outburst from conservationists, but in 1965 the redevelopment went ahead. Similar replacements of the Life Association building, dated to 1855, and the neighbouring New Club, originally

OVERLEAF.

Princes Street in the 1950s with the ornate North British and Mercantile Office. The open view to the south from the street has been defended only with great difficulty on occasions over the years, but the garden grounds are now one of the glories of central Edinburgh.

1834 and extended in 1859, were other conservation battles lost, changing the shape of Princes Street at the foot of the Mound westwards.

Then came a change of mind on the part of the planners, and all existing façades had to be preserved.

LIFE ASSOCIATION

The Life Assocation building was erected on the site of three adjoining houses at 81, 82 and 83 Princes Street, just to the west of the foot of the Mound, bought to allow the prospering company to expand from its corner block at 2 Hanover Street. The old houses, one a four-storey building with attics, were demolished and the architects employed by the company, David Rhind and Sir Charles Berry, designer of the Houses of Parliament, came up with an impressive building in the Venetian Renaissance style for the head office, which opened in 1858.

It was one of the proudest buildings, incorporating Methven and Simpson on the ground floor, ever to grace Princes Street, and when it was proposed in the 1960s that it should be demolished, the full weight of Edinburgh's conservationist lobby swung into an unsuccessful campaign to preserve it from redevelopment which at the time was thought to set the pattern for a 'new' Princes Street with its first-floor-level balcony. It was demolished in 1967.

NEW CLUB

The neighbouring New Club, originally built in 1834 by William Burn and extended in 1859 by David Bryce, was another highly regarded building. The Tax Office was originally at No. 84 and, together with its neighbour at No. 85 it became the club site. It, too, fell to redevelopment in the 1960s, to the dismay again of the conservationist lobby. In the rebuilding of the club in 1966, the architect Alan Reiach incorporated panelling from the original dining room, together with some other reminders of the old club. One of Bryce's massive urns from the former roof has also been retained as a decorative feature.

OPPOSITE.
Conservationists fought vigorously to prevent the demolition of the splendid Life Association building in Princes Street from the 1960s developers. But to no avail. In the same era the North British and Mercantile Office also vanished from the street.

NORTH BRITISH AND MERCANTILE

This was the third major battle in the Princes Street redevelopment furore of the 1960s. Among its admired features was the statue of St Andrew on its frontage. In 1965 British Home Stores rose on the site, the first of the rebuilding projects to follow the Princes Street Panel guidelines. It was designed by Kenneth Graham, of Robert Matthew, Johnson-Marshall & Partners.

PALACE HOTEL

The five-storey-high 1888 block at the corner of Castle Street was regarded by some experts as worthy of its place in the street because of its distinctive and picturesque silhouette. It was destroyed by fire in 1990 and was replaced by an office and shopping block which set a fresh style for Princes Street as it was the first entirely new building in the street for many years.

C & A

The original C & A store was destroyed in a spectacular fire in 1955 and a new shop front and interior was constructed the following year. The store closed in

The 21st-century face of Princes Street. At the head of the Waverley Bridge a completely new store was built on the site of the C & A building heralding a change of policy by the planners to allow new frontages. The only recent exception to the rule of building behind an existing façade was the construction of the block at the foot of Castle Street when the Palace Hotel was destroyed by fire in 1990s, but now there are several new facades.

The C & A building was itself relatively new in Princes Street, having been erected to replace the store destroyed in a spectacular fire in 1955. The fashion store closed in Edinburgh in 2001.

2001 and the building was demolished. The new store on the site, incorporating an adjoining building, opened in the spring of 2005. Apart from the Palace Hotel site, where a new structure had to go up on the cleared ground after the demolition of the fire-damaged builing, this was the first break from the rule of preserving the old façades.

ROBERT MAULE'S

This family-run department store graced the west end of the street until the 1930s, when a new store arose on the site. That was Binns, now Frasers, dating to 1935. In 2005, the House of Fraser announced the take-over of the street's grand old lady, Jenners.

Many of the once-familiar shops are gone, and senior Edinburgh citizens will still recall the days when businesses such as Darling and Co., the silk mercers run by the kenspeckle Sir Will Y. Darling, one-time Lord Provost; Mackie's; R. and T. Gibson, the grocers, with their Balmoral Restaurant; Methven Simpson; Macvitties Guest and R. W. Forsyth graced the street. No Stewart's the hairdresser, no Marcus the furriers, no Melrose's tea shop, no Jamiesons the fruiterers, no Fifty Shilling Tailors.

There seems little doubt that commercial pressure particularly will see much of the early 21st-century Princes Street lost in the next few years, perhaps with the remaining original houses swept away.

ST JAMES' SQUARE

The one other major project in which James Craig was involved after the New Town was St James' Square, the ground of Multrees Hill and Clelland's Park. It was a housing development with solid stone tenements and an ornamental garden and was the city's first attempt at a unified terrace design, something Craig also introduced to his layout for Merchant Street, off Candlemaker Row.

It was a substantial and impressive centre of housing, advertised when the ground was feued as 'dry, healthy and commands pleasant and extensive views' and 'being outwith the royalty, is free from all the Taxes, Imposts and Burdens to which the inhabitants within the limits of the City of Edinburgh are subject ...' There was also plenty of clay and sand on the ground 'for making bricks', the advertisement added.

The Square was built between 1775 and 1790, and alongside ran Leith

St James' Square, at the eastern end of Princes Street, was designed by James Craig, the New Town planner, in 1773. But by the middle of the 20th century many of the homes were condemned for human habitation and the square, which by then included many commercial uses, was obliterated in the 1960s in a redevelopment which included the formation of the St James' Centre shopping complex, completed in 1970.

OVERLEAF.
The faded grandeur of St James' Square as seen from above with the garden feature. Only one of the tenements designed by James Craig still stands at the top of Elder Street.

Street with its terrace, a simplification of a proposal by the great architect Robert Adam, who had envisaged a three-storey colonnaded terrace.

By the 20th century, the Square had a mixture of housing and commercial use, and was earmarked in the 1949 Civic Survey as a site for a Festival Centre, with a civic theatre and concert hall – 'the principal front should be the one overlooking the terraces which offer a magnificent view of the Firth of Forth.'

Much of the housing had fallen into the critical slum category, unfit for human habitation, and it was obvious by the 1960s that the Council had to

The new St James' Square – as seen by Abercrombie and Plumstead in the Civic Survey of 1949. They envisaged an International Festival centre and an opera house on the hill occupied by the old tenements. Had that scheme gone ahead it would have saved Edinburgh years of wrangling to provide a theatre capable of satisfactorily staging opera and ballet.

tackle the problem. Proposals for the St James' Square Comprehensive Development Area were approved by the Secretary of State for Scotland in 1963.

The solution was a brutal one – demolition of the entire square, apart from one of the original Craig tenements – and the erection of the St James' Centre, a covered shopping precinct, boosted by a major store and hotel and New St Andrew's House, offices for Scottish civil servants.

The Leith Street terrace was also taken away along with the north side of the street, and the redevelopment was completed in 1970. Shops on the other side of the street were closed as part of the conditions attached to building the new centre, and further down the street the tenements stretching almost to the Playhouse, including an 1800 block, latterly the Imperial Hotel, were also lost to make way for part of an inner ring road, which never materialised, to cope with the rising tide of city traffic.

Slums in the Greenside valley between Leith Street and Calton Hill were also cleared. Leith Street was a bustling shopping precinct in its own right, and the shops which were lost to their loyal customers were household names: Littlejohn's the bakers; Fordyce, military tailors; Maxwell's, confectioners; Hardys and Co., furniture shop; Alexander Fairley and Son, coaches, cars and taxis; John McRae, butchers; and so many others, including a range of gents' tailors and Jerome's photographic studio. The triangle of housing and shops at the top of Broughton Street, Union Place and Picardy Place was also removed to be replaced in time by the traffic roundabout at the foot of Leith Street.

There for a while stood Edinburgh's most remarkable and controversial monument – the Kinetic Sculpture. From 1973 to 1983, this metal tower with 96 coloured light tubes 'adorned' the roundabout. Frequently, the lights failed to work. It became a sculpture of ridicule, and this most bizarre of pieces was not greatly missed when it was dismantled and, it is said, stored in a Council yard. It may still be there.

The loss of the Square meant another big change in that part of the New Town because fire had again played a part in a major shake-up on the northeast corner of St Andrew Square. In Clyde Street stood the St Andrew Square Picture House until November 1952, when it was massively damaged in an inferno. This site, together with that of a nearby furniture storehouse also hit

New St Andrew's House soars above the St James' Centre and into the skyline. Looming over the eastern view along George Street, its massiveness has attracted adverse criticism since it was completed. Now it stands empty after the Scottish Office staff who worked in the building moved to what is now the Scottish Government block in Leith Docks.

ABOVE.
*Housing in Greenside behind Leith Street and below the Calton Hill was judged
unfit for human habitation and earmarked for clearance.*

OPPOSITE TOP LEFT.
*The distinctive Leith Street Terrace, which was one level up from Leith Street itself, was an
attractive feature and was incorporated into the plan for the street in the 1780s. The only principal
similar terrace remaining is Victoria Terrace above Victoria Street, off George IV Bridge.*

OPPOSITE TOP RIGHT.
*The most derided monument ever to be erected in the town was the kinetic sculpture which stood
on the traffic roundabout at the junction of Leith Street, Broughton Street and Picardy Place. The
coloured fluorescent tubes suffered technical problems even at the switch-on ceremony in 1973 and
after a decade of public ridicule the sculpture was finally taken down.*

OPPOSITE BELOW.
*The bus station in St Andrew Square in 2000, the second station on the site where the
St Andrew Square Picture House stood until it was destroyed by fire in 1952. A further station has
now been formed with the redevelopment of the ground between Elder Street and
St Andrew Square, and featuring Multrees Walk.*

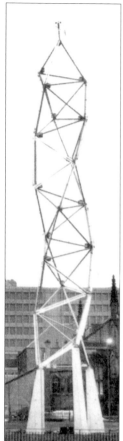

by a serious fire, became the bus station. The first station had a columned archway exit facing St Andrew Square, and the buses entered from Elder Street. It was later rebuilt, and in 2003 another bus station was completed. Harvey Nichols and a line of upmarket shops in what has been named Multrees Walk were built on part of the former bus station ground.

LIGHTS DIMMED

The St Andrew Square Picture House is only one of the lost cinemas in Edinburgh. The city had taken to the moving picture performances from its earliest days, with the first use of the Kinetoscope at Moss's Christmas Carnival in the Waverley Market in 1896. Before that, it is likely that moving picture shows were presented in a fairground booth in Iona Street, off Leith Walk.

Early cinemas came and went, often little more than cellars, the 'flea pits', or small basement rooms, but before long many were firmly established fixtures.

The Edinburgh and Leith Post Office Directory for 1944–5 lists the following well-remembered picture houses in the professions and trades category:

Alhambra Theatre, Leith Walk
The Astoria, Manse Road, Corstorphine
The Blue Halls, Lauriston Street
Caley Picture House, Lothian Road
The Capitol Theatre, Manderston Street, Leith
Eastway Cinema, Easter Road
The Grand, St Stephen Street, Stockbridge
The King's Cinema, Home Street, Tollcross
The New Picture House, 56 Princes Street
Palace Picture House, 15 Princes Street
The Playhouse Super Picture Theatre, 20 Greenside Place
Poole's Synod Hall, Castle Terrace
Regent Picture House, Abbeymount
Roxy Cinema, Gorgie Road
The Rutland, Canning Street
St Andrew Square Picture House, Clyde Street
Salon Picture House, Baxter's Place

But that is not a complete list. It did not include the New Victoria in Clerk Street (closed in 2003 and currently awaiting a new future behind its Art Deco frontage), the Regal in Lothian Road, the Ritz in Rodney Street – all very popular rendezvous for filmgoers – and many others such as the Dominion at Church Hill.

Of the above, only the Dominion and the King's are still active, the latter as the Cameo. The Regal became the ABC complex; it was demolished at a turn-of-the-century redevelopment of the Lothian Road, Morrison Street and Semple Street corners, and was rebuilt and reborn as the Odeon.

The other picture houses mentioned are closed, and the Playhouse has become a theatre, and playing its part with major Edinburgh Festival performances. There were four cinemas in Princes Street at one time, the first being the Picture House which opened at No. 111 on 20 July 1910. Designed by a local architect R. H. Cameron, it featured a tea room and a smokeroom. The front had mock Grecian pillars and there were stained glass panels in the kiosk. With a capacity of only about 500 in the auditorium, it was on the small size in Edinburgh cinema terms, and it closed in 1923.

The Lotus and Delta shoe shop moved in, and in the 1960s transformation of Princes Street the site was redeveloped for John Menzies, the newsagents, and that building now houses a fashion store.

The Princes opened at No. 131 in September 1912. Better known as the Monseigneur News Theatre after a refit in 1935, it had a third lease of life as the Jacey from 1964 until the last flicker in May 1973. Now the frontage is part of the HMV record store.

Third on the scene was the New Picture House at No. 56, which opened in October 1913. It was formed out of the banqueting hall of the Mount Royal Hotel and featured a dramatic marble decor – white in the entrance hall and green in the tearooms. The architects, Atkinson & Alexander, designed one tearoom with a Wedgwood theme, another in Louis Quatorze style. Going to the 'flicks' was definitely an occasion in a posh Princes Street picture house.

The New closed in May 1951 and its site was redeveloped for Marks and Spencer.

The plushest of them all in the street, however, was the Palace, at the east end of the street. Its opening on Christmas Eve 1913 was excitedly awaited and R. M. Cameron was again the architect. The then staggering amount of £9000 was the cost of the Georgian-style, stone-fronted building. Its hall had heavy white Sicilian marble columns and the frontage had four fluted pilasters and a triple light oriel window. It also boasted smoking rooms and the celebrated Wedgwood Cafe, a popular meeting place.

*The Jacey created created quite a stir when it replaced the Monseigneur News Theatre at 131
Princes Street. The renamed cinema started showing Continental films, but like so many picture
houses in the city its days were numbered and it closed in 1973.*

The Palace lasted until February 1955, when it was bought by the then
adjoining F. W. Woolworth to expand its shop, which was done the following
year. There is now no trace of the cinema today, and Woolworth has long since
departed Princes Street as well.

When it was launched in December 1911, the Coliseum at 125 West
Fountainbridge was the largest in town. Converted from a skating rink by R. C.
Buchanan, it had 1,800 seats. It became the New Coliseum and was run in
conjunction with the Palais de Danse. The cinema closed in 1942 and part of the
auditorium was the foyer of the Mecca Social Club, housed in the old dance
hall. What will become of the old Palais is now uncertain.

The adaption of premises to form cinemas, before purpose-built ones

Once one of the most palatial cinemas in town, the 1913 Palace Cinema at the east end of Princes Street, was bought by Woolworths, who had a store next door. The Georgian-styled cinema vanished in the redevelopment, and Woolworth itself is gone from the street.

came along, is typified in the history of what most Edinburgh people would remember as the Grand in Stockbridge. The site at 99 St Stephen Street was in 1895 a skating rink and ice store, and by 1901 the Tivoli Music Hall had opened there, becoming soon afterwards the Grand Theatre, with theatrical shows and occasional films.

By 1909 the theatre had a change of course, however, becoming home to the Edinburgh Horse Repository and Riding Academy, but on Hogmanay 1920 it reverted to a full-time cinema and continued that way for 40 years, with the last films shown in May 1960.

It became a bingo hall, ballroom, Cinderella Rockafellers' club and then, after a fire, was derelict before being demolished to make way for a stretch of flats.

Another Stockbridge cinema to meet a similar fate was the Savoy in St Bernard's Row. An organ builder's and then a billiard saloon were there before the Palace Cinema opened in April 1911. It was renamed St Bernard's Picture Palace the following year and in 1921 became the Savoy. Its final name was the Tudor from 1960 until its demise in 1966. It was demolished in 1982 and replaced by a small tenement by Kantel Design with distinctive V-shaped balconies.

Neither will you find the Rutland, latterly Gaumont, in Canning Street now. A supercinema, designed by T. Bowhill Gibson, it welcomed its first customers in April 1930, closed for two days in April 1950 to reopen as the Gaumont, and ran until a disastrous fire destroyed the building in May 1963. It was subsequently demolished, and the 1967 13-storey Canning House, by Gavin Paterson & Son, rose from the ashes. That office block has recently had a facelift and been designated Exchange Tower.

Another fire casualty, mentioned earlier, was the St Andrew Square Cinema in Clyde Street. From New Year's Day 1923 until it was destroyed in a blaze on 12 November 1952, it was a popular city-centre venue for film fans. The site was sold and became part of the bus station, which has subsequently been rebuilt as part of the 21st-century regeneration of part of the east side of St Andrew Square.

The flashy art deco entrance to the former New Tivoli in Gorgie Road is still there, although the cinema, designed by James McKissock, of McKissock & Son of Glasgow, is now a social club, having also been a bingo hall – a fate which befell several cinemas struggling to survive in the 1970s and 1980s. Bingo, too, was the last throw for the Poole's Roxy, much further west in the same street at No. 430. Its striking frontage, designed by Chadwick Watson & Coy, a Yorkshire partnership, is still to be seen, however, with modern housing behind. Opened in December 1937 for the Poole family in Edinburgh, it showed its last film in the same month in 1963 and became a bingo hall for some years before the demolition of the former cinema building, apart from the façade, and the creation of new homes.

Housing fills the place where the Ritz (1929–81) stood in Rodney Street, before its demolition in 1983; nor is there any trace of the Regent in Abbeymount. Its main front was formerly part of Younger's St Anne's Brewery, and its conversion to a cinema was designed by T. Bowhill Gibson. Its closure came in 1970, and the building eventually fell derelict and was demolished, its site now being part of a car showroom and workshop complex.

The Lyceum in Slateford Road, on the south-west corner of Robertson Avenue, featured a high façade in its design by the architect Charles Mitchell.

It showed films from its opening in November 1926 until turning into a bingo hall towards the end of 1959. After being vandalised by fires in 1963, the building was sold and demolished. Leggate and Co.'s garage and showroom used the site for a number of years, before it was cleared again for the present corner housing block.

Fire and constant vandalism were also factors in the closure of the Embassy, one of the suburban cinemas, in Boswall Parkway, East Pilton, in March 1964. Designed by James Miller and operating from August 1937, the building was demolished in 1975, a supermarket then appearing at its location.

Another suburban attraction was the Astoria, in Manse Road, Corstorphine – also a T. Bowhill Gibson piece of architecture. It lasted from 1 January 1930, until the screen dimmed for the last time on 29 June 1974. Despite efforts to preserve the structure for community use, the picture house was demolished and a supermarket moved in.

The skeleton of the old Salon clung desperately to Baxter's Place at the top of Leith Walk, more than 40 years after the last reel was shown.

The Caley, at 31 Lothian Road, was opened to herald New Year's Day 1923. Its architects, J. S. Richardson and J. R. Mackay, brought a luxurious look to its

The sad frontage of The Salon Cinema in Baxter's Place near the top of Leith Walk.
At its opening in 1913 the male staff wore turbans and the women attendants sported dancer
costumes, giving the picture house the nickname of 'The Harem'.

The End came for the ABC Film Centre at the corner of Lothian Road and Morrison Street in 2001. Known as the Regal when it opened in 1938, it expanded into a cinema complex in 1969. The newly built Odeon Film Centre occupies the site now.

interior as befitted a city-centre playhouse. Although films were still being shown into the 1980s in conjunction with musical events, it is now a night-club, its exterior very distinctly still reflecting its original purpose.

The future of another once-great cinema building is still in doubt in 2005. The New Victoria (later the Odeon), in Clerk Street on the south side, was spectacular, with the auditorium designed to represent a Greek amphitheatre, with colonnade, statues and Corinthian columns. The architect, W. E. Trent, also incorporated a star-lit ceiling. When the first audiences came along in August 1930, filling the 1999 seats, they would be entertained by an orchestra, as well as watching the latest movies. Later, a Wurlitzer organ, which rose into view, was used to provide musical interludes. It was renamed the Odeon in the mid-1960s and became a multi-cinema complex in 1982.

Since its closure in 2003, there has been local concern about the redevelopment of the site, which stretches through to Buccleuch Street. The former cinema's art deco façade is listed, so that at least should survive as one of the best reminders in the city of the glory days of cinema-building and picture-going generally.

Local readers will have their own memories of many other cinemas in their own neighbourhood which provided hours of happy entertainment, especially to youngsters for whom the Saturday-morning matinee was a weekly 'must'.

And as the Edinburgh cinema historian Brendon Thomas reflected: 'Surviving cinema buildings, whether in use as cinemas or not, are clearer vestiges of that glory – mannered magnificence in the Caley, modernism in the George, Portobello, and classic but camp elegance at the Odeon. Cinema buildings come in a farrago of styles and their study can be an introduction to many schools of architecture – classical, Gothic, the variously "historical". Most closed cinemas, if not actually demolished, have become furniture showrooms, supermarkets, bingo halls and banqueting suites.

'But even a piece of pink plasterwork in a supermarket, a cornice or

The Tabernacle occupied the site of the present Playhouse in Greenside Place, at the foot of Leith Street. It was a Baptist Meeting House until 1864, and was used as a furniture store before being demolished in the 1920s.

entablature on a shopfront or a quirk of decoration in a club, indicates to the alert eye that there once passed this way a thousand fantastic films.'

TABERNACLE

Standing on the site of the Playhouse was the former Tabernacle in Greenside Place. Originally a Baptist Meeting House, it was used for worship between 1801 and 1864 and could accommodate as many as 4,000 on special occasions.

The congregation moved to found Duncan Street Church, and the old hall became a furniture warehouse, being cleared to make way for the Playhouse, which opened in 1929 with an auditorium capable of seating 3,048 patrons. It was originally designed as a dual-purpose hall, suitable for music and theatre, but became prominently a cinema before assuming its present role.

CHAPTER 15

CHURCH LIFE

Just as Edinburgh's cinema buildings have undergone great change, so have its churches.

Three great church buildings dominate the skyline above the ridge of the Old Town. In descending order, from west to east, they are the Highland-Tolbooth, St Giles' Cathedral and the Tron Kirk. Only one, St Giles', the High Kirk of Edinburgh, is still a place of worship, maintaining its link back to the first small church on the site in the 12th century at least, and possibly as far back to the parish church of 'Edwinsburch' recorded in 854.

In the New Town, one of the most eye-catching sights, especially at dusk, is the splendour of the giant dome of the former St George's Church, on the western side of Charlotte Square.

Together, the three former churches represent the magnificence of style of the 17th and 19th centuries, which has ensured, sometimes with a struggle, that great temples of worship can retain their outward former glory and provide a practical utilitarianism in the 21st.

The mighty Tolbooth Church dominates Castlehill and the upper Lawnmarket. The Gothic structure was by James Gillespie Graham, who also laid out the Earl of Moray's grounds to provide one of the finest New Town developments in the land above the Water of Leith, and A. W. N. Pugin. It was designed not simply as a church but also as the meeting place of the General Assembly of the Church of Scotland. Its 241-foot (74m) high steeple is still

OPPOSITE.
St Giles' has an imposing presence in the heart of Edinburgh with its renowned crown spire an instantly recognisable feature of the skyline. For centuries there was a clutter of buildings round the old church, and they were finally swept away in the 19th century as the High Kirk of Edinburgh, as it is now, was itself remodelled and extended. The last major addition was the Thistle Chapel, on the south-east side of the building. It was designed by Sir Robert Lorimer as a chapel for the Order of the Thistle, Scotland's highest order of chivalry, and completed in 1911.

The former St George's Church in Charlotte Square is now West Register House, where part of the National Archives of Scotland are housed. The church building was designed by Robert Reid, whose plan superseded that of Robert Adam (shown above), the designer of the square.

topped by a golden cross, but it is many years since a sermon was preached there. After extensive interior renovation by the architect Benjamin Tindall, it is now called The Hub, and is the swish and welcoming headquarters of the Edinburgh International Festival, its indoor and outdoor cafe/restaurants providing a popular eating place.

Its construction between 1839 and 1844 meant the demolition of many old houses at the foot of Castlehill, including the sweeping away of Stripping Close. By popular belief, backed by Robert Chambers, it got its name because it was there that malefactors were stripped to the waist before being whipped through the streets by the hangman down to World's End Close at the bottom of the High Street.

The Tron Kirk has been described in an earlier chapter, and while it, the Highland-Tolbooth and St George's have all lost their original purpose, they have been saved from the fate that often awaits empty buildings – demolition. It is hard to imagine that the removal of the Tron building to open up the High

Street/Bridges junction was mooted seriously when the congregation moved out, but there were also murmurings that St George's might be a candidate for knocking down. When extensive structural faults were discovered in the late 1950s, it was the ideal opportunity to create a new traffic flow into Queensferry Street, some said. But, as in the case of the Tron, wiser counsels prevailed.

Robert Adam laid out and designed Charlotte Square, but died in 1792, many years before it was completed. He left plans for the church, having drawn them in 1791. When the time came to start the project, however, the task fell to Robert Reid to adapt the Adam proposals, and he produced a simpler but nevertheless spectacular version. Reid gave an 'off the wall' estimate of £18,000 for the new church, but it rose to £23,675 before it opened in 1814, three years after the foundations were started.

After the mid-20th-century problems, the Ministry of Public Buildings and Works (R. Saddler) in 1964 began its conversion into West Register House, where part of the Scottish archives can be consulted. The St George's congregation were united with St Andrew's Church of Scotland in George Street.

Many former churches in the city are certainly 'lost' in one way but enjoying a new lease of life and playing an important role in the life of the community.

The Morningside Free Church in Morningside Road, for instance, is now the Church Hill Theatre. Its distinctive bold Renaissance style in pink sandstone reflects the instructions of the original congregation to the distinguished church architect, Hippolyte J. Blanc, in 1892. It served the members well until its closure and in 1965 was converted by the Town Council into a neighbourhood theatre, particularly popular for amateur and Festival Fringe productions.

Just down the road at Holy Corner, the North Morningside United Presbyterian Church, at the junction of Morningside Road and Chamberlain Road, is also in community use as the Eric Liddell Centre – named after the great Scottish athlete and missionary. Designed by David Robertson, it was built in neo-Norman style between 1879 and 1881. The congregation eventually joined with Morningside United Church, across the road, and the then disused church was converted into the centre.

Another complex involving a theatre was created by the Church of Scotland in the Netherbow Centre in the High Street, after the demolition of the Moray-Knox Church. The centre itself was renovated in a major way in 2005.

Community centres have been formed in several other disused churches. The Abbey Centre is based in Hippolyte J. Blanc's 1895 Kirk Memorial in

Montgomery Street; Dalry Church (Sydney Mitchell & Wilson 1908) in Orwell Terrace is now St Bride's Community Centre; James Gillespie Graham's Nicolson Street Church (1820) is the South Side Community Centre.

Theatres seem a popular option in the renaissance of church buildings. Edinburgh University's Bedlam Theatre was created in the former New North Free Church, at the junction of Bristo Place and Forrest Road. A Thomas Hamilton building of 1846–8, with its front door looking north into George IV Bridge, it did not find general favour in the congregation, who deemed it 'an ugly and inconvenient church'. Still, unlike many other church buildings, it nevertheless survives to this day.

Another entertainment complex has been created in David Bryce's original United Associated Synod Church in Lothian Road, which was converted between 1978 and 1981 into the Filmhouse. Better known as Lothian Road Church, it was built in 1830–1 and considerable internal alterations were made in its conversion into a film centre by the Walter Jamieson Partnership.

The Queen's Hall in South Clerk Street is another example of a successful conversion, this time to a popular concert hall. It was called the Hope Park Chapel of Ease when it was built to Robert Brown's design in 1823 and was later Newington and St Leonard's Church.

A dramatic 21st-century remodelling has turned the former Holyrood Free Church in Horse Wynd, directly opposite the Scottish Parliament, into the magnificent Queen's Gallery, where prize exhibits from the monarch's collection are shown in special exhibitions. The simple Gothic church by John Henderson has stood there since 1850 and has a very welcome new lease of life as a prime tourist attraction at the foot of the Royal Mile.

Two city-centre casinos are based in former churches. St George's Episcopal Church in York Place was designed by James Adam and dates to 1792–4. When the church amalgamated with the later St Paul's at the corner of York Place and Broughton Street, the box pew used by Sir Walter Scott went there, along with some other artefacts. St George's, originally castellated Gothic in style and virtually a copy of the 1789 St Bartholemew-the-Less in London, served as a warehouse for many years with the front being altered in 1934 to provide display windows.

The other church casino is the old St Thomas's in Rutland Place, at the start of Shandwick Place. David Cousins designed the neo-Norman building, which went up in 1842–3. After closure, it was a heritage centre for some years, and now it houses gaming rooms.

Other churches have been turned into upmarket bars – the original Martyrs' and St John's, later the Elim Pentecostal Church, in George IV Bridge,

A transformation has given new life to the former Newington and St Leonard's Church in South Clerk Street. Now the Queen's Hall, it is has been one of Edinburgh's most popular concert venues.

The fine Victorian interior of Dublin Street Baptist Church, which was demolished and replaced by an office block in the 1980s. The congregation moved to the church's former mission hall at Canonmills.

has gone that way. Charles Leadbetter, the architect, could never have dreamed of such an outcome for his 1859 building. St John's, in Victoria Street is another, although one architectural description of George Smith's 1838–40 effort is 'less like a church than three bays of a Jacobean country house'. That perhaps is what makes it all the more inviting to its present-day customers.

It is relevant to mention that even more popular for conversions to bars and restaurants are the myriad of former bank and insurance offices which have been vacated over the past few years. Just look at George Street.

Money certainly changes hands also in the Greek Doric Broughton Place Church, at the east end of the street. It is now an auction house. Built in 1820–1 as a United Associate Synod Chapel, it became in due course a Church of Scotland place of worship, but ended up being surplus to ecclesiatical require-ments due to various congregational unions. The ongoing church unions over the years have been one of the major causes for buildings to be disposed of by congregations or church authorities, and while many have been successfully converted, others have simply been demolished and their sites redeveloped.

You will not, for instance, find Barony and St James with its once-familiar clock tower at the corner of Albany Street and Broughton Street. Originally St Mary's Free Church when it opened in 1859, it was hauled down to be replaced in 1983 by offices designed by the David Le Sueur Partnership in 1983, but the former manse still stands.

The Dublin Street Baptist Church (1856–8 by Keddie & Kinnear) was replaced by a fine office block after the congregation converted its former mission hall at Canonmills to a church in the 1980s. In McDonald Road, off Leith Walk, the 1894 Hardy & Wright St James' Church was replaced by more housing; McDonald Road Church site has a furniture store on it; and the former Salvation Army hall ground housed a garage workshop. In 2007 a housing development replaced the garage.

Perhaps the building, or frontage, which has evoked most comment in Edinburgh over the past couple of decades or so was the Lady Glenorchy's Low Calton Church in Greenside Place, close to the Playhouse. When property in Leith Street was demolished and the church itself was to be removed it was a condition that the 1846 Tudor façade should be preserved and incorporated into whatever was built on the site. For years, the front wall, all that remained, was propped up by a metal support. Now it forms the entrance to a brand new hotel and provides an interesting reminder of what once stood there.

There are many other examples throughout the city of past and present changes to former churches and a total list would be very long indeed, but the buildings are generally easy to identify. Empty or derelict church sites continue

The Glasshouse Hotel in Greenside Place has incorporated the frontage of the former Lady Glenorchy's Low Calton Church. It was a condition of the demolition of the church that the 1846 façade be retained and incorporated into what was finally built on the site. For many years a steel framework supported the stonework before the hotel appeared.

to be very attractive to developers – in 2005, housing was built behind the façade of Guthrie Memorial Church (1881) in Easter Road, designed by Charles S.S. Johnston.

One last word on church buildings. In the 2003 dramatic fire which destroyed many buildings in the Cowgate and on South Bridge above, what was saved from the flames was the old Cowgate Free Church (Patrick Wilson 1859-60). It was used for many years as the Wilkie House Theatre, and became a night club. Its name is Faith.

CHAPTER 16

DOWNS AND UPS

The Edinburgh skyline changed spectacularly in the second half of the 20th century as the Council set out to tackle probably the major challenge facing it – to provide decent housing for those living in sub-standard or condemned property in conditions not far removed in some instances from those found 100 years earlier in the Cowgate slums which so exercised Lord Provost Chambers. Shared lavatories on the landing, sometimes still a common sink or even a water tap in the backgreen, leaking roofs, ill-fitting windows – conditions for too many people were bleak, unsavoury and unhealthy.

An immediate relief came just after the Second World War with the supply of temporary housing on various sites. Prefabricated bungalows – universally known as 'prefabs' – were the goverment solution to give a quick fix to authorities up and down the land to cope with the housing demands. The prefabs, with fully-equipped kitchens and bathrooms, were generally warmly

TOP.
Slum clearance became a major challenge to civic leaders in the 20th century, and one of the areas which changed dramatically was St Leonard's and Dumbiedykes on the edge of Holyrood Park. Appalling housing conditions spurred the Council to remove the crumbling stone tenements here and in many other parts of the city, replacing them in some instances with multi-storey flats, some of which themselves are now being replaced.

BELOW.
Holyrood Road – the former South Back of the Canongate – has been transformed over the past few years with the clearance of brewery property to make way for the Scottish Parliament building.

OVERLEAF.
Carnegie Street, just off the Pleasance, was a bleak-looking place in 1958 with the stone tenements deemed unfit for human habitation. Many of the houses were neglected by landlords. Roofs and windows leaked, there were shared toilets on the landings, and many lived in 20th-century squalour. Something had to be done and the bulldozers soon moved in.

accepted by those lucky enough to be allocated one. Indeed, at Moredun, you can still see some of the prefabs, which were designed to have a life of no more than 20 years. The 1960s saw a step-up in the drive to clear away the slums, mostly traditional stone-built tenements round the city centre and in Leith.

What happened in St James Square, Leith Street and Greenside was reflected in many other areas. Another major attack was made in the St Leonard's and Dumbiedykes area, resulting in the demolition of appalling houses in places such as Salisbury Street, Brown Street, Heriot Mount and Holyrood Road, all part of the Arthur Street Comprehensive Development area.

Carnegie Street, off the Pleasance, and surrounding dingy properties were swept away. Memories of the collapse of the 'penny tenement' in Beaumont Place were always strong among the councillers and Council officials. It was a run-down block which the landlord offered to the Council for one old penny. They rejected it, and one night the building collapsed.

Rows of packed houses went in the 1960s – India Place and the surrounding streets on the banks of the Water of Leith at Stockbridge, 500 houses there being regarded as the worst in Edinburgh at the time; Jamaica Street, lying between two prestigious New Town streets – Heriot Row and Royal Circus; part of Nicolson Street; Earl Grey Street and Riego Street at Tollcross; parts of the High Street and Canongate; Newhaven Village; Wilkie Place, the Kirkgate and the Citadel in Leith.

Prefab schemes at South House, Niddrie Marischal, Muirhouse and other districts were replaced with modern flats and houses.

The multi-storey block returned to the town where they were once commonplace on the north and south slopes of the Royal Mile ridge. The first went up in Gorgie in 1952, and within ten years there were high-rise towers at Slateford, Blackhall, West Pilton, Spey Street off Leith Walk, Gracemount, Colinton Mains, Muirhouse and Leith.

The then highest blocks – two 21-storey towers – were ready for occupation at Leith Fort in September 1963, marking the 20,000th post-war house built by the Council.

The multi-storeys at Dumbiedykes, where a multi-million-pound refit was started in 2004, were taking tenants in 1963 also.

The 'daddy' of them all was the 23-storey-high block in Muirhouse, not lost when the Council gave it up, but now a private enterprise for those who enjoy skyscraper living.

The Leith Fort multi-storeys are gone now – emptied of tenants disenchanted with the social and other problems of living in such a dense environment, and the concrete edifice has been razed.

The development of huge estates – following on the pre-war examples of the likes of Craigmillar, designed to provide for many householders cleared from earlier slums, also in the St Leonard's/Pleasance area and then post-war – saw what had been countryside or farming land devoured. The last major local authority estate at Wester Hailes meant the old farm steading was swallowed up and resulted in the disappearance of part of the Union Canal, which was culverted below ground from Kingsknowe to Calder Road.

What was lost has now reappeared with the Millennium Project to make the canal navigable from Edinburgh to Falkirk, and a new waterway runs through Wester Hailes, where, like so many other Council estates, older houses have been pulled down as they came to the end of their useful lives and new ones have been built, often by private enterprise or housing association partnerships.

The private developers have also changed the landscape of Edinburgh, trying to meet the seemingly endless demand for new homes within a prosperous city. Increasingly, this has resulted in much former industrial or commercial ground – or 'brown-field sites' – being used for housing. Old warehouses and plants have been transformed and been saved from being added to the lost list.

One of the other ways in which the private sector has found ground is to purchase a substantial villa, standing in its own grounds, get planning permission to demolish and then redevelop, primarily with blocks of flats to utilise fully the land potential.

ROCKVILLE

One of the prime examples of this approach saw the removal of one of Edinburgh's most distinguished houses in an act of what many people regraded at the time as architectural vandalism.

The house was Rockville, which stood at the corner of Napier Road and Spylaw Road in Merchiston. Called affectionately 'The Pagoda', 'The Chinese House', 'Tottering Towers' or 'Crazy Manor', it was built by the Victorian architect and engineer Sir James Gowans as his home.

The square house, standing in substantial grounds with its own lodge, was three storeys high, with a tower in the south-east corner, adorned by a cupola and spire which gave an oriental effect, hence 'The Pagoda'. Gowans paid great attention in his design to the windows and to the narrow chimney heads, and the use of a variety of stone – old granite rocks, fossil, quartz and brown or crop

Victorian architect and engineer Sir James Gowans built his Merchiston house Rockville in an idiosyncratic style, but it was much admired and became a feature at the corner of Napier Road and Spylaw Road. It incorporated many examples of different stones and its general appearance attracted the nickname of 'The Pagoda'. Despite vigorous public protest, it was demolished by a building firm in 1966 to make way for flats.

rock. The external walls were built in a chequer-board pattern to reflect the attractiveness of the various stones, while the lodge house was an equally attractive piece of building – 'the deep reddish-ochre of its rubble infill was brilliant in conception; the overall effect of lightness and sparkle provided an excellent contrast to the sombre richness of Rockville'.

It was a project which excited architects of the time and was used by Gowans as a prototype for later houses in Edinburgh, Dundee and West Lothian.

When, in the mid-1960s, the proposal to demolish Rockville became public, an outcry arose and a petition to save it was signed by 2,500 protesters. To no avail – it was demolished in 1966 and flats went up in its place.

FALCON HALL

A distinguished house in the nearby Morningside area went in 1909. Falcon Hall stood at what is now the junction of Falcon Court and Falcon Road West, the main entrance being from Morningside Road. Lying in 18 acres of ground between Newbattle Terrace and Canaan Lane and with its lodge entrance gate in Morningside Road, the mansion house was originally built as Morningside Lodge in 1780 for William Coulter, who was to become Lord Provost.

After his death in 1810, it was purchased by Alexander Falconar who added a fine façade and changed its name to Falcon Hall. On either side of its entrance doorway were statues of Nelson and Wellington, then very popular war heroes.

By 1889 it had become a boys' boarding school. The last owner was John George Bartholemew, of the cartographer's, and when Falcon Hall was demolished, its pillared façade was rebuilt at the firm's Duncan Street frontage. Carved falcons from the mansion house grounds are on the pillars at the entrance to the zoo at Corstorphine. The hall's site is now covered by tenements and later 20th-century flats.

One of the city's grand houses, Falcon Hall, was surrounded by 18 acres of ground off Morningside Road and was originally built in 1780. Extended by a later owner, it stood until 1909.

Grange House had a long pedigree, with its land being connected to St Giles' Kirk from as far back as the 12th century. Bonnie Prince Charlie was a visitor in 1745 when it was a tower house, and in the 19th century it was converted and extended in baronial style. Its end came after it fell into disrepair, and demolition started about 1936.

GRANGE HOUSE

The architect Thomas Hamilton – the former Royal High School in Regent Road is his work – was commissioned for Falcon Hall, and another renowned architect was William H. Playfair, who, between 1817 and 1831, turned the old tower house of the Grange of St Giles', which was visited by Bonnie Prince Charlie, into the baronial Grange House when it was owned by Sir Thomas Dick-Lauder, who started the feuing of the Grange estate for house-building.

Around 1936, when the house in Grange Loan became ruinous, it was pulled down, ending a history which could be traced as far back as the 12th century to the lands related to the kirk in the High Street.

CAMMO HOUSE

Cammo House, with its estate on the western side of Edinburgh, was another place with a long pedigree, its origins going back to the mid-14th century, when the grounds were possessed by the Bishop of Dunkeld. The estate passed through various hands, and in 1693 Robert Mylne, of the family of master masons, was employed to build a new house. The house underwent various changes and in time it was bought by Mrs Margaret Clark-Tennent in 1896, after renting the property for a year. She changed her name to Maitland-Tennent about the time of her divorce in 1910 and spent the rest of her long life in Cammo with her son, Percival. She became known as the 'Black Widow' because of her reclusive nature and the dark, old-fashioned clothes she customarily wore.

After her death in 1955, the estate fell to Percival, but the house was becoming rundown and neglected. It was attacked by vandals and thieves, and in 1977 two fires caused extensive damage, resulting in its virtual demolition in two stages in 1979 and 1980. Its grounds now form a wildlife park in the care of the City of Edinburgh Council, which was gifted the remains of the house and grounds by the National Trust for Scotland, to whom Percival had left the estate.

In 1964 West Warriston House at Eildon Terrace, Inverleith, was another

Cammo House is now a stump, but in its prime it was a fine house with origins reaching back to the mid-14th century. The estate grounds now form a wildlife park.

West Warriston House was demolished with the development for housing of its grounds in Inverleith Place.

once-stately mansion to fall into ruin. It was a 1784 example of the suburban villa which rose at the same time as the terraced houses of the New Town, and was originally built by a wealthy banker, William Ramsay. The villa of East Warriston House, on the east side of Warriston Road behind Warriston Cemetery, was converted in 1929 by Sir Robert Lorimer to the present crematorium. The house was built for another banker, Andrew Bonar, in 1808.

Saughtonhall, an eye-catching house with a lengthy pedigree, was destroyed by fire in 1952 – this time a deliberate one. The mansion was in such a state that its destruction was authorised as an exercise for the Fire Brigade.

Parson's Green House, a mansion in Considine Terrace on the slopes of Holyrood Park, was another 20th-century casulty, as was the Braid Farmhouse or Upper Braid, close to the junction of Braid Farm and Braid Hill Road. It was formerly the country residence of the judge, Lord Monboddo.

CHAPTER 17

JAILHOUSE BLUES

CALTON JAIL

When the Town Council was looking at a new prison to replace the Old Tolbooth in the High Street, the first choice was on ground in Forrester's Wynd, behind the then new Parliament House buildings. The 'new jail' was to be built to a design prepared by Robert Reid, and all seemed acceptable. The Council resolved that the foundation stone be laid with full masonic honours on Thursday 18 September 1808. The ceremony was carried out, watched by thousands of spectators.

But no building seemed to take place after the stone was laid, and in November 1813 the Commissioners of the New Jail received a report from William Rae, Sheriff-Depute of the County of Edinburgh, objecting to the proposed site, which was basically where the National Library for Scotland stands today.

It was too small an area of ground for a jail, he argued. Fresh air would be blocked by public buildings on the north and east and it would be overlooked also by high tenements on the south and west.

Rae suggested other options: on the Castlehill, if the Government was prepared to allow the banks of the Nor' Loch to be used for such a purpose; Ramsay Garden, close to Ramsay Lodge, although he considered again that the space might be too limited there; and Calton Hill.

But there was only one site to his mind – on part of the sloping bank on the south side of Princes Street between the Mound and Canal Street, the thoroughfare which ran below and parallel to Princes Street.

The Commissioners agreed that the site originally proposed was 'highly objectionable' and said the Sheriff's report was 'well worthy of attention'.

It was soon made clear that the site below Princes Street would not win favour with the populace, and in 1814 an Act of Parliament was passed

authorising the erection of 'a National Jail on the south side of the Calton Hill'. Archibald Elliot was commissioned to design the building which would go alongside the detention centre already on the side of the hill.

Some years earlier, the craggy outcrop of the lower reaches of Calton Hill – the Dow Craig – was selected for a new Bridewell. The foundation stone was laid in 1791 and the building replaced when it was completed in 1796 by the House of Correction in the Canongate, which held 'the strolling poor and loose characters'. The Bridewell, five storeys high with a hospital on its uppermost floor, had a great architectural pedigree, having been designed by no less a personage than the renowned Robert Adam, the master planner of Charlotte Square.

The Old Tolbooth was still the town jail, although housing in its latter days mainly debtors and the condemned awaiting execution. Prison was not much used as a punishment in olden days. Justice was pretty rough and ready – slicing off an ear, branding at the Cross, scourging or execution. Thirty days in jail was not really an option. The spectacle of a man with his ear pinned to the Mercat Cross or having his tongue skewered for some calumny is something we are only too happy to have seen pass away in Edinburgh.

It was 1817 before the first prisoners were sent to the Calton Jail, which had the address One Regent Road, alongside the Bridewell, and that was the death knell for the historic Old Tolbooth, which was demolished shortly afterwards.

The new prison had its ground floor divided into seven compartments, each containing a day room and a courtyard, and there was a house for the governor. Of the seven compartments, one was an infirmary. Women prisoners, debtors and untried men were assigned to three others, and the remaining three were used by convicts. In the upper storeys were the night cells, ranged along both sides of long galleries. In the condemned cell, prisoners under sentence of death were fastened by chains to a long iron bar fixed in the wall.

OPPOSITE TOP.
The Calton Jail had a prestigious address – No. 1 Regent Road. It replaced the Old Tolbooth as the town's jail, incorporating the Bridewell, which had been built on the side of Calton Hill between 1791 and 1796.

OPPOSITE BELOW.
The new jail received its first prisoner in 1817 and in its existence of more than a century seven men and one woman were executed there for murder. With the construction of Saughton Prison in the 1920s, the Calton Jail closed its doors for the last time in March 1926. Only the governor's turreted house remains, and the jail site is now occupied by St Andrew's House.

After the last public execution at the head of Libberton's Wynd in 1864, murderers met their judicial fate in the Calton Jail, seven men and one woman being hanged there. Ostensibly, the executions were not in public, but spectators would climb Calton Hill, from where they could look into the prison yard and see the last moments of a condemned person. In later years, the executions were carried out inside the building, free from the bloodthirsty spectators' stare, and the sign that it was all over was the flying of a black flag.

The jail was replaced in the 1920s by Saughton Prison, purpose-built on the then outskirts of town, and it was closed finally in March 1925.

Various options were suggested for the empty building – an Army headquarters for troops stationed in Scotland; the National Library; a Sheriff courthouse, and even a new City Chambers. At the end of the day, however, it was demolished, with the exception of the governor's distinctive circular tower house which overlooks Waverley Station. The site was too valuable to leave empty, and St Andrew's House, described as 'by far the most impressive work of architecture in Scotland between the wars', was built between 1936–9 as the Scottish Office. Now, the ministers of the Scottish Government have their offices there, together with civil servants, and the Scottish Government building is on part of the Leith Docks area.

The governor's house was proposed for clearance under the St Andrew's House plan, but it was felt worthy of keeping – a reminder of the grimmer building which once occupied the crag. Now, Scotland's First Minister is eyeing the old house for his official residence, in place of a Charlotte Square town-house.

Portions of the original jail site off the High Street were eventually built on with the clearance of Forrester's Wynd and other old property. A lock-up for criminals, a new Advocate's Library and a new Sheriff Courthouse fronting George IV Bridge were formed.

CHAPTER 18
OUT OF FASHION

GEORGE SQUARE

The formation of George Square was the first major development outside the royalty of the Old Town, a slick enterprise by builder James Brown, who nipped in to feu the lands of Ross Park from the Council, which seemed to have underestimated the potential of the lush acres round Lord Ross's old mansion house.

Brown bought 26 acres for £1,200, and when the Council realised it had made a big mistake it tried to buy it back from him. He said he would gladly sell for £20,000, an offer the Council quickly rejected.

Brown used the experience he had gained in creating Brown Square, where the houses he had built were 'deemed fine mansions, and found favour with the upper classes'.

The Ross Park ground enabled him to build to a much more spacious plan 'and in a superior style both as to size and accommodation'. Ross House itself came to be used as a lying-in hospital.

The square was started in 1766 and grew quickly in popularity, attracting many of the leading gentry and gentlewomen to the splendid houses round open ground which was to be turned into an ornamental garden. One of the conditions on buying a property was that the householders would enclose and lay out the garden and keep it 'in good order, and in an ornate manner'. Neither were the square's residents to engage in 'any trade or merchandise' from their houses, nor were they to bake or brew for sale.

The last houses, on the south side, were occupied by around 1785, and it was said that to be invited to dine in George Square was a social cachet of the highest standing in the town.

Among the residents was the feared Lord Braxfield, whose reputation as a 'hanging judge' made him one of the fiercest figures on the Scottish bench. He

was, however, acknowledged by his contemporaries as a fine lawyer and his habit of speaking in old Scotch and his often flippant yet frightening remarks to the accused – 'Ye wad be nane the waur o' a hanging' – only enhanced his reputation for judicial brutality.

That aspect was encouraged by Cockburn, writing about a man he never saw in action in the courts. 'Strong built and dark with rough eyebrows, powerful eyes, threatening lips, and a low growling voice, he was like a formidable blacksmith. His accent and his dialect were exaggerated Scotch; his language, like his thoughts, short, strong and conclusive!' Later assessments of Braxfield – the inspiration of Stevenson's 'Weir of Hermiston' – have concentrated on his skill as an advocate and sound judge.

Braxfield, however, feared no one, and would stroll home from Parliament House to his George Square home, by way of the High Street and Cowgate closes, without any thought of needing a bodyguard. Even at the height of the highly charged political trials over which he presided as Lord Justice-Clerk in 1793–4, never for a moment did he consider he was in any danger.

Braxfield also presided over the court which heard the trial of Deacon Brodie and George Smith in 1788, and it was he who pronounced the sentence of death on both those housebreakers. Brodie was the two-faced character – respectable businessman by day and thief and gambler by night – from whom Stevenson got the idea for his characters Jekyll and Hyde.

The square continued as a sought-after residential quarter amid the growing South Side. Cockburn says:

> The whole fashionable dancing, as indeed the fashionable everything, clung to George Square where in Buccleuch Place, close by the south-eastern corner of the square, most beautiful rooms were erected,

The Old Assembly Room in the West Bow was probably the first public dance hall in the town. Dancing has always been a popular pastime in Edinburgh and it enjoyed a particular boom in the 20th century with many private ballrooms and dance academies operating.

which, for several years, threw the New Town piece of presumption (the Assembly Rooms in George Street) entirely into the shade.

His description of a dance makes an interesting comparison with that earlier one outlined by Goldsmith in the Old Assembly Room in the West Bow. In the Buccleuch Place rooms 'were the last remains of the preceding age'. He tells us:

Martinent dowagers and venerable beaux acted as masters and mistresses of ceremonies, and made all the preliminary arrangements. No couple could dance unless each party was provided with a ticket prescribing the precise place in the precise dance. If there was no ticket, the gentleman, or the lady, was dealt with as an intruder, and turned out of the dance. If the ticket had marked upon it – say for a country dance the figures 3.5; this meant that the holder was to place himself in the third dance, and fifth from the top; and if he was anywhere else, he was set right, or excluded. And the partner's ticket must correspond. Woe on the poor girl who with ticket 2.7, was found opposite a youth marked 5.9!

It was flirting without a license, and looked very ill, and would probably be reported by the director of that dance to the mother. Of course parties, or parents, who wished to secure dancing for themselves or those they had charge of, provided themselves with correct and corresponding vouchers before the ball day arrived. This could only be accomplished through a director; and the election of a pope sometimes required less jobbing.

When parties chose to take their chance, they might do so; but still, though only obtained in the room, the written permission was necessary; and such a thing as a compact to dance, by a couple, without official authority, would have been an outrage that could scarcely be contemplated.

Tea was sipped in side-rooms; and he was a careless beau who did not present his partner with an orange at the end of each dance; and the oranges and the tea, like everything else, were under exact and positive regulations.

All this disappeared, and the very rooms were obliterated, as soon as the lately raised community secured its inevitable supremacy to the New Town.

The first big alteration from purely residential use came with the building of George Watson's Ladies' College on the north side in 1870s. The square was also one of the sites examined for a concert hall after William Usher indicated he wanted to endow such an addition to the city. Eventually, a site off Lothian Road was chosen and the Usher Hall built between 1910–14.

The University of Edinburgh started using houses in the square from around 1897, converting them into halls of residence, and that sparked a pattern of acquisition and occupation that led to the square being described by a leading architect in the 1930s as a university campus.

After the Second World War, George Square became the focus of intense and at times emotive debate as the university sought to redevelop it – in some plans demolishing it completely and rebuilding – and the Town Council sought to find a balance between the new road schemes it wanted to introduce, plus nearby slum clearance and other developments. At one time, the university promoted the idea of a Comprehensive Development Area in which a new campus could be formed on the land from the Middle Meadow Walk to the Pleasance and would incorporate commercial and housing aspects along with

Parkers store stood at the corner of Bristo Street and Chapel Street, but it fell to the
University of Edinburgh's redevelopment plans for the George Square area and for Council
road-widening. Southsiders, particularly, mourned the store's demolition in 1971.

OPPOSITE.
A distinctive tenement in St Leonard's Street was called 'Castle o' Clouts', apparently
after a tailor who was thought by his neighbours to have pretensions above his station by
living in such a house. The 'castle' is gone now, another victim of the much-changed
St Leonard's area.

the new buildings the university itself would need. That scheme was, however,
abandoned in 1973.

After fierce initial opposition, the university found that its plans to replace
at least part of the original houses in George Square were accepted, however
reluctantly. A new library and the David Hume and Appleton Towers were
completed in the 1960s, to give the square the look it has today. The library and
David Hume Tower meant neat and sturdy houses were lost, while the
Appleton Tower soars where tenements stood in Crichton Street, Chapel Street
and Windmill Street, demolished in 1963.

One other familiar South Side building was also caught up in the redevelopments which meant reshaping the roads round Bristo – Parkers store, which
stood at the corner of Bristo Street and Chapel Street. In 1971 it joined the list of
those buildings which had fallen to the demolisher's hammer, and with it went

the happy shopping days of so many who remember the creaking floors of the picturesque structure.

Another South Side curiosity was the quaintly named Castle o' Clouts at 104 St Leonard's Street, standing beside the entrance to the Park Brewery. Three storeys high with an attic, it carried a date of 1724, and the ground floor was remodelled as a public house with flats above. It is suggested that the 'castle' was built by a tailor, called Hunter, possibly in a style grander than might have been expected for such a tradesman, and because, of course, he dealt in cloth, locals derided his pretensions by calling his house 'Castle o' Clouts'. A clout is the Scots word for a piece of cloth.

CHAPTER 19

CURTAIN DOWN

When the Theatre Royal was taken down in Shakespeare Square, the same name was transferred to another theatre at the top of Broughton Street.

The area had long been associated with theatrical ventures, including concert rooms run by Natali Corri which were converted into a theatre. It was known as the Pantheon, the Caledonian and finally the Adelphi.

The Adelphi was destroyed by fire in 1853, the first of several which were to damage successive theatres there. The Adelphi was reopened as the Queen's Theatre and Opera House, and after the Shakespeare Square theatre was closed it took the 'Royal' name.

But the Theatres Royal were all ill-fated. In 1865 six people died when fire ripped through the building, causing a wall to collapse. The Royal was rebuilt, but in 1875 fire again struck, leaving only four bare walls. Again, a new Theatre Royal rose from the ashes, only to be badly damaged once more in 1884.

The curtain finally fell in March 1946, when the Theatre Royal yet again caught fire shortly after the end of a show headed by Tommy Morgan, a popular Scots comedian.

Because of post-war building restrictions, and then because the derelict site was likely to be part of the expected redevelopment of the St James' Square area behind, the shell stood untouched for many years. In 1956, however, St Mary's Cathedral, which stood next to the theatre, acquired the ground for an extension and to open up the approach to the church.

Yet another spectacular theatrical fire in 1911 caused 11 deaths when the Empire Palace Theatre in Nicolson Street was devastated. The famous illusionist Lafayette (the American Sigmund Neuberger), one of the highest paid and most popular entertainers of the time, was among the dead. His grave is in Piershill Cemetery.

Previously, the Nicolson Street area had seen circuses and the Royal Amphitheatre, and another attraction was a riding school. The Empire was rebuilt, and after various refurbishments is now the dramatic glass-fronted Edinburgh Festival Theatre.

The list of lost theatres stretching back to Allan Ramsay's short-lived playhouse in Carrubber's Close in 1736 is substantial and includes the Tailors' Hall in Cowgate, which was used for 18th-century entertainments. The very fine tenement frontage to the hall was taken down in 1940, and the old hall buildings, latterly used as a brewery, underwent a recent restoration and transformation into a hotel, restaurant and bar complex.

Among old theatres were the Garrick, Grove Street (closed in 1921); Operetta House, Chambers Street (1906) and another Operetta House in Waterloo Place (1878); Southminster (1877) and the Princess Theatre (1881), both in Nicolson Street.

Some theatres doubled as cinemas when the new art form became popular, and in the second half of the 20th century two of those were still running as variety theatres – the Gaiety in the Kirkgate in Leith, which kept going until 1956, and the Palladium, originally a circus, in East Fountainbridge, which closed in 1966.

Although not strictly within the scope of this book, because it was in Leith, mention should be made of the Alhambra Theatre in Leith Walk, which was a variety hall when it opened in 1914 before becoming a picture house, very popular with Leithers, and indeed with citizens at the other end of the Walk. One of its claims to local fame was that it had the only two privately owned street lamps, the first mercury vapour lamps installed, in the area. Its distinctive pillared frontage finally vanished in 1974, although demolition permission had been granted as far back as 1960.

The Gateway Theatre, in Elm Row, had also started life as a cinema before becoming the much respected home of the Gateway Theatre Company. In fact, before it became Pringle's Picture Palace, named after its owner, in 1908 it was a roller skating rink It became the Atmospheric Theatre in 1929–30, still a cinema, and from early 1931 was known as Pringle's Theatre, with roadshows being the main feature. Used by various theatre groups in the 1930s, it was renamed the Broadway in 1938.

In 1946 the building was presented to the Church of Scotland, becoming the Gateway and opening as a cinema/theatre. Eventually, it was renowned as the home of the theatre company which bore its name. The theatre was closed in 1965, the property becoming the studios for Scottish Television and later a drama centre for Queen Margaret University College.

The great theatrical drama in the city was the fight to provide a proper venue for opera, particularly during the Edinburgh International Festival. The site finally earmarked, after the St James' Square and Festival Centre proposal in the 1949 Civic Survey was not pursued, was the Poole's Synod Hall, in Castle Terrace. A new theatre there, capable of staging opera and other big productions, would have been adjacent to the Royal Lyceum Theatre and the Usher Hall, effectively creating a long-dreamt-of Festival centre.

POOLE'S SYNOD HALL

The whole business of finding a site for an opera house was a drama in itself, and included the demolition of the Synod Hall, which, although best known as a cinema, also housed a host of offices and activities, including a shooting range in the basement.

Designed by Sir James Gowans – he of the Rockville House – it opened in 1875 as the New Edinburgh Theatre, but collapsed into bankruptcy. It was bought by the United Presbyterian Church in 1877 and given the name Synod Hall. The Poole family opened a picture house and it became one of the best-known of all the town cinemas, before it closed in 1965. The Synod Hall was

The Synod Hall in Castle Terrace was probably best known for the cinema operated there by the Poole family. Opened in 1876 as a theatre, it became the Synod Hall for the United Presbyterian Church, and the name stuck. Demolished to make way for an opera house which never materialised – a hotel was also proposed for the site – for many years it was an infamous 'hole in the ground' until the building of Saltire Court closed the book on one of Edinburgh's lost opportunities.

demolished, along with the original School Board and Parish Council offices, in an effort to bring the opera house saga to a head and to encourage its building.

However, the opera house scheme was abandoned amid much bitter wrangling and criticism, and for years the Castle Terrace gap was one of the city's infamous 'holes in the ground' before Saltire Court rose on the land. The Festival centre concept was, however, strengthened by the new Traverse Theatre, which moved from its home at the foot of the West Bow to purpose-built premises beside the Usher Hall.

TWINKLING FEET

If theatre and cinema-going were popular in the 20th century, coming through strongly again after various setbacks including a drop in audience numbers, many people found much more enjoyment in dancing. As we have seen, the assemblies of old were conducted on pretty rigorously disciplined lines, but with new styles of music and a new liberation from previous inhibitions so dance classes and dance halls flourished.

In 1920, the Grafton Assembly Rooms, later Maxime's, opened in West Tollcross; Mrs Cameron Walker's 'Superior Assembly' was in the York Hall in Picardy Place; Val's dancing hall was on Portobello Promenade; there was the Crown Ballroom in Lothian Street; and the Leith Central Ballroom opened in 1921.

Dance enthusiasts flocked to the Palais-de-Danse at Fountainbridge when it opened on Christmas Eve 1920, shortly afterwards advertising afternoon and evening sessions. It boasted: 'A buffet lounge, tea rooms, dancing partners, bewildering surprises, wonderful new musical dance selections, brilliant flashlight illuminations, gorgeous decorations and fantastic stunts.' It closed for dancing in the 1967–8 season.

In 1926 along came the Plaza Salon de Danse in Morningside Road (now a Waitrose store after its 'last waltz' on 1 March 1975).

Among the other ballrooms was a small establishment at 38 Raeburn Place, later called the Palais de Plaisir. There was also a dance hall at Happy Valley, Craiglockhart, now developed as a sports centre.

The Kosmo Dance Club in Swinton Row, off Elder Street, gained notoriety when it was raided by the police after surveillance by a determined officer, Sergeant William Merrilees, convinced that more than dancing was being provided in the premises. The manager, Asher Barnard, was subsequently jailed for 18 months for living off immoral earnings. 'Wee Willie' Merrilees, who went on many years later to become Chief Constable of the Lothians and Peebles force, also raided Maxime's in 1938, following allegations of homosexual behaviour there.

It closed and reopened as the Cavendish, a short-lived enterprise, which was reborn as the New Cavendish, and later became a disco and nightclub.

MARINE GARDENS

One of the most popular entertainment centres in Edinburgh was the amusement park at Marine Gardens at Portobello.

Some businessmen anxious to cash in on the success of the Scottish National Exhibition at Saughton Park in 1908 felt that many of the specially created buildings could be preserved and used elsewhere. Thirty acres of land to the west of King's Road and stretching along Seafield Road were taken over, buildings were transported to splendidly laid-out grounds with wide pathways, and its opening in May 1910 was boosted by a long hot summer which attracted thousands of visitors to the seaside resort.

Families could arrive by tram or rail, and the entertainment included the Al Fresco Theatre and the Empress Ballroom. The amusement court featured

The Marine Gardens entertainment complex, off Seafield Road, Portobello, was immensely popular before the First World War offering all sorts of attractions to lure customers. But only the Empress Ballroom survived war-time use by the military, although the sports stadium was also re-opened. The Second World War, however, saw the end of the Marine Gardens complex, and a Lothian Buses depot occupies the site today.

a scenic railway, and the concert hall provided a wide range of musical entertainment. The gardens also incorporated a zoological park, with Bostock's Zoo housing a wide range of animals.

Special attractions, well advertised in advance, included Daredevil Cormack, who dived from a 70-foot-high tower into a small tank of water, and a hot-air balloonist, whose speciality was floating into the air and then jumping by parachute into the sea.

The amusement park closed in September 1914 at the outbreak of the First World War and only the ballroom survived, the other buildings being demolished by the War Department for military purposes. The dance floor provided billets for troops and needed considerable refurbishment before reopening to dancers. It retained a great popularity until the Marine Gardens were again requisitioned during the Second World War.

The sports stadium on the garden site had also reopened after the First World War, attracting speedway as well as traditional football. The now defunct Leith Athletic played some of their home games there.

There is now little trace of the Marine Gardens complex, which did not survive the 1939-45 war, the noise of bus engines having long drowned out the happy cries of seaside entertainers and their audiences and the music of the big bands which set the feet a-tapping. Lothian Region Transport's bus depot and garage occupy the ground now.

All the dance halls suffered, like the cinemas, from the effects of television, and a switch from the more formal ballroom dancing to different styles, particularly among the younger generation, which have never replicated the great boom of the 1920s, 1930s and 1940s.

Among other once-familiar dance halls now gone were the Excelsior Ballroom, Niddry Street; Glendinnings, Pilrig Street; New Dunedin, Anchor Close; New Locarno Ballroom, Slateford Road; Royal Gymnasium Halls, Fettes Row; Silver Slipper Ballroom, Springvalley Gardens, Morningside; while the Waverley Market and the Drill Hall in Forrest Road also hosted regular dancing. The Assembly Rooms in George Street continued to be the home of the formal ball.

PORTY POOL

There is no sign of what was another big attraction for Edinburgh's seaside resort – Portobello Open Air Pool. With its main entrance on the Promenade, near to where the Figgate Burn runs into the sea, it was opened in May 1936

Portobello Open Air Pool and the adjoining power station were very much part of the seaside scenery. When it opened in 1936 many must have wondered at the wisdom of an open-air pool, considering Edinburgh's frequently inclement summer weather. But it survived until 1979, when the Council decided it was no longer viable. The power station was closed in 1977.

and proved immensely popular, despite Edinburgh's notoriously fickle summer weather. The water in the pool – 300 feet by 90 feet, with seating for 6000 spectators – was boosted by a warm stream from the nearby Portobello Power Station, which closed in 1977 and was cleared away in 1983. The warm water, however, seemed to stop being pumped into the pool a few years earlier, as its loss is mentioned in a Council report for 1970–1.

One of the pool's extra thrills was the wave-making machine, which turned the normally placid water into a sea, much to the excitement of the

ABOVE.
Haunt of thousands of youngsters (and adults) in the summertime, Portobello Open Air Pool boasted a wave-making machine among its attractions. And when the sun shone on Porty, there was no better place.

LEFT.
The great lum of Portobello Power Station soared above the beach.

thousands of youngsters and adults who enjoyed jumping through the waves. Had an economical way of roofing the pool been found, it might still stand today, but the complex closed in 1979 because of a gradual fall-off in the number of swimmers which had restricted its summer opening weeks, and because of increased maintenance costs, together with the impact of all-the-year-round facilities at the Royal Commonwealth Pool, built for the 1970 Commonwealth Games in Edinburgh.

Demolition came in 1987, and Portobello lost a valuable facility. An indoor bowling centre and five-a-side football pitches on the pool's ground have at least continued its leisure use, while the power station gave way to housing.

PORTOBELLO PIER

Another former lure for visitors to Portobello was the pier, constructed in 1870–1 at the foot of Bath Street and stretching over the sands more than 300 yards into the Firth of Forth. At its end was a pierrot theatre, and steamers took passengers across the Forth or down the east coast, a diversion for day trippers from the donkey rides which were a feature of the attractions on the bustling beach. The pier was dismantled in 1917, when it was deemed unsafe after damage caused by a heavy storm.

An earlier pier in the Forth was known as the Old Chain Pier and was suspended over four wooden towers from Trinity, not far from Newhaven Harbour. It also ran out into the Forth, and had a gymnasium at its end. Its fate was sealed when most of the structure was swept away in a great storm in 1898.

The beach at the seaside resort of Portobello was always well packed, with the pier and its pierrot theatre at the far end offering holiday-makers and locals plenty of laughter and music. The pier was dismantled in 1917.

CHAPTER 20

MILE OF CHANGE

The Royal Mile, which had seen constant changes over the centuries, continued to see further alterations in the 20th. A new location was needed to replace the Sheriff Courthouse on George IV Bridge, and it was found at the foot of the Lawnmarket by demolishing the tenements of Galloway's and Dunbar's Closes between Bank Street and St Giles' Street. The 'grim Neo-Georgian' courthouse, built between 1934–7 by H.M. Office of Works, has been converted into the High Court, and a new Sheriff Court was built in Chambers Street, stretching at the back down to the Cowgate level.

The courthouse on the bridge was cleared to provide a place for the National Library of Scotland, of which only the steel frame was constucted by 1939. The war years prevented any further progress, and the library was not completed until 1955.

The corner of Melbourne Place and the Lawnmarket, which had suffered when George IV Bridge was first formed, faced another onslaught when Midlothian County Council wanted an office block opposite its Council buildings. The tenements, which included the renowned Ferguson's Rock factory and shop and the Royal Medical Society hall, vanished in the name of progress and expediency in 1969 to make way for what in the eyes of many was the worst modern intrusion into the Royal Mile. There is new thinking in the City Chambers now, and Council leaders are backing a proposal for its demolition and replacement by something more sympathetic to the character of the street.

The ancient thoroughfare from the Castle to the Palace has been much altered in its lifetime, although still maintaining its ancient shape. Much restoration work has been carried out to save property which might have been lost.

Patrick Geddes, in the late 19th century, argued successfully that derelict tenements in the back courts of the Lawnmarket should be pulled down to open up those areas, and that the surviving tenements could be used as good

Edinburgh's houses spread down the Castlehill and into the Lawnmarket as the town started to grow, and from the Lawnmarket the road extended into the High Street at St Giles' and to the eastern end of the old town at the Nether Bow Gate.

living accommodation. He was responsible for a new tenement, too, in Wardrop's Close in the 1890s, which gave a new frontage to that part of the street.

The City Chambers extension of the 1930s brought an end to Allan's, Craig's and Old Post Office Closes, and to one side of Anchor Close. Extensive remodelling on the south side of the High Street later in the century cleared away a lot of derelict property and provided a new home for the Museum of Childhood and flats for city-centre dwellers.

At the very top of the Royal Mile, the former reservoir has been turned into a highly successful tourist attraction as a tartan weaving centre, now incorporating a shop for the Edinburgh Military Tattoo. The first tank was formed to contain water piped four miles from Comiston in 1681, and its overall measurements were 43 feet in length, 28 feet in breadth and 6 feet in depth. It held about 220 tuns (216 gallons per tun) of water, and was apparently of great interest to visitors, to whom it was proudly shown. To cope with the ever-increasing demands in the 19th century, a new reservoir was needed. Thus, in 1849, the old tank and an adjoining mansion house were removed and a much larger one was erected, and was in use by February 1852. It continued in operation until the 1990s.

THE CANONGATE

What to do about the lower section of the Royal Mile – the Canongate – was something which regularly exercised the minds in the City Chambers after City Architect MacRae submitted a detailed report in 1945 on the condition of buildings there, with a follow-up two years later. Inevitably, progress was slow, although priority was given to removing the worst of the slums.

'Where condemned property had been evacuated and closed, it was in such a depressing state of disrepair as to be near ruin; for example, Shoemakers' Close, Bible Land and Morocco Land, part of the last having collapsed in ruins in March 1947 after standing empty for 18 years,' was the woeful report from the Rev. Dr Ronald Selby Wright, Minister of the Canongate Kirk, in the *Third Statistical Account* in 1966.

Although from an historical and architectural point of view there was still a feeling of romance, too many of the buildings were crumbling into ruins through lack of care or attention; and for the inhabitants of the still-tenanted closes and tenements, historical interest in no way compensated for the lack of the basic necessities of making a comfortable home.

Morocco Land, recognisable by the half-length figure of a Moor on its façade, was rebuilt between 1958–6 in a style which attempted to restore the atmosphere of the old Canongate, an idea which was also applied to other buildings further down the street. Shoemakers' Land and Bible Land were extensively reconstructed behind their fronts while the old Golfer's Land was rebuilt completely.

GOLFER'S LAND

The traditional story about the old irregularly-shaped tenement, built in the 17th century, concerns the golfing prowess of John Paterson, a lowly Canongate shoemaker.

The Duke of York, later James VII, was visiting Edinburgh when he was

OPPOSITE.
Said to have been built by John Paterson with his winnings from a golf match on Leith Links, Golfer's Land was a typical Canongate tenement. In the 20th-century redevelopment, Golfer's Land was reconstructed and a plaque on the building now records Paterson's feat, which was also noted in Latin on a stone tablet in the tenement's back garden.

challenged by two English noblemen, like himself, keen golfers, to a match. They offered him the choice of anyone as his partner for the foursome. After careful consideration and doubtless judicious sounding out to find the best possible partner, he selected Paterson, who was recognised as the finest golfer in the town, a descendant of other enthusiasts of the game.

The contest took place on Leith Links, with heavy stakes being wagered by the Duke and the Englishmen – 'and after a keen contest the royal champion of Scotland and his humble squire carried the day triumphantly'. Paterson was given a generous share of the winnings by the delighted Duke and built a substantial house, with its gable onto the street, which still commemorates his victory.

A bronze plaque on the front of the reconstructed building – the old tenement went in 1960 – celebrates his success, depicting a hand clasping a golf club and the motto 'Sure and far'. That is the dream of every golfer who ever swung a club. There is also an inscription – 'I hate no person' – a creative anagram of John Paterson.

Holyrood Brewery was one of the many sitting between the Canongate and its South Back (now Holyrood Road). It was a flourishing quarter of the town, bustling with the great business of producing beer for both home and export consumption. The vast Abbey and Holyrood Breweries of William Younger; Younger's cooperages and maltings at Moray Park, Lochend, and at Canonmills; the brewery at Croft-an-Righ; the brewing houses in Craigmillar, and at many other sites in the town have mostly disappeared. One or two of the brewery buildings have been converted into housing. Even the huge Fountain Brewery at Fountainbridge closed in 2005, presenting a site of rich development potential likely to attract a host of developers.

The opportunity was taken in the Canongate reconstruction work to reintroduce the arcaded passageways below some of the buildings, bringing back that once-common feature of old Edinburgh houses. Where possible, old parts of the tenements were kept and incorporated into the new, but much was unquestionably beyond saving and was consequently lost.

In the area at the foot of New Street, once a row of stately houses close to the top of the Canongate, the huge red-brick bus garage was built in 1927. It stretches down to the old South Back of the Canongate (Calton Road) and replaced the gas works with its great chimney, so long a landmark. Gas production was being centred on Granton as the 20th century started and full production began on the foreshore in 1906. The Granton gas works have themselves gone, along with two of the three landmark gas holders.

A gas company, in which Sir Walter Scott had an interest, was formed at Tanfield, on the banks of the Water of Leith at Canonmills, but it was taken over by the Edinburgh Gas Light Company in 1828 and latterly all that remained was Tanfield Hall, incorporated into the modern Standard Life offices.

The New Street garage is, at the time of writing, part of a redevelopment plan which will almost certainly see the distinctive but not particularly attractive building disappear.

BREWERY LANDS

Between the Canongate, where once-extensive gardens stretched down to what is now Holyrood Road, the old South Back, industry flooded onto the beckoning ground, particularly breweries, which found the fresh water they needed for their ale readily available beneath their feet. William Younger had established his company in 1749 at a little brewery in Leith, and after his death, his son, Archibald Campbell Younger, opened his own brewery in the precincts of Holyrood Abbey, where the 12th-century monks were excellent ale-makers. From small beginnings, the family business expanded steadily with a growing export trade to boost home sales.

The Abbey and Holyrood Breweries continued to grow, and in 1930 Youngers merged with another local brewery firm, Willian McEwan and Company, founded at Fountainbridge in 1856, and formed Scottish Brewers, which, after further amalgamations, became the giant Scottish and Newcastle.

Before the Second World War Edinburgh had no fewer than 23 breweries in full production. You will still find drinkers in the older Edinburgh pubs who

can recall the distinctive ales produced by Campbell, Hope and King, from the Argyle Brewery in Chambers Street and the Cowgate (part of the Tailors' Hall); Deuchar's, at the Duddingston Brewery, Craigmillar; Drybrough's; Lorimer and Clark's Caledonian Brewery at Slateford; William Murray, at their Craigmillar plant; Thomas Usher, whose Park Brewery was in St Leonard's; Robert Younger's, at St Ann's in Abbeyhill and also at Craigmillar. Folk will lift a glass and toast them all.

By 2005 there were only two major producers left. But Scottish and Newcastle then closed its Fountain Brewery at Fountainbridge and transferred most of its production south of the Border, although it has bought the independent Caledonian Brewery in Slateford Road to keep a production plant in the city.

The closure at Fountainbridge, where part of the brewery site took in the North British Rubber Company on the banks of the Union Canal, will free up a vast acreage of land, stretching from the canal to the Western Approach Road, and another distinctive whiff on the Edinburgh air will be all but lost – the smell of beer-making.

The Canongate site was vacated by the brewers a number of years ago, and has already undergone extensive change, with blocks of flats, hotels and the Scottish Parliament building.

On the south side of Holyrood Road, where stood other extensive property owned by Younger and McEwan, the exhibition centre of Our Dynamic Earth now draws visitors. Another once-familiar sight lost there is that of the gasometers.

OPPOSITE TOP.
The site of the Scottish Parliament building in 2000, when the Spanish architect Enrique Miralles was still talking about a design inspired by upturned boats and leaves and complementing its surroundings of Holyrood Park and Salisbury Crags.

OPPOSITE MIDDLE.
The Scottish Parliament building, now operational – it was officially opened by the Queen in 2004 – and still highly controversial after its multi-million pound budget overrun took the final costs in excess of £400 million. Praised by many, sneered at by others, it is becoming one of Scotland's most noted architectural icons.

OPPOSITE BELOW.
An industrial heritage passes into memory. Where three gas holders stood at West Granton now only one remains as a reminder of the halcyon days of the Granton Gasworks. W. R. Herring, who designed the gasworks in 1898, planned a row of eight gasholders with a steel frame, but only one in his style was built. The demolished two were built in 1933 and 1966.

CHAPTER 21

END OF THE LINE

A vast transformation has also taken place in the railway lands stretching westwards from Lothian Road towards Haymarket. The ground where the financial centre, Sheraton Hotel, Western Approach Road and the International Conference Centre are now, clattered only a few decades ago with steam engines, carriages and wagons going in and out of the Morrison Street yards and the Princes Street Station at the west end of the street.

The Caledonian Railway Company first built a terminus in Lothian Road before developing it to the full Princes Street Station, called locally 'the Caley', which opened in the 1890s. The hotel was built above and around it.

When the Caledonian Railway Station was formed in 1869 at the foot of Lothian Road, it meant the end for the old Kirkbraehead House and part of the south side of Rutland Street, which was developed along with Rutland Square from the 1830s.

Among the other buildings which had to go to make way for the power of steam was St George's Free Church, built in 1845 on the north-east corner of what was then Cuthbert's Lane, now part of Rutland Street. The church, however, was carefully dismantled and rebuilt in Deanhaugh Street, Stockbridge. It has subsequently been turned into housing, retaining its distinctive pyramid spire.

Demolished with the station's coming was the riding school, along with the Scottish Naval and Military Academy, with a 'plain but rather elegant frontage'. It trained young men chiefly for service with the East India Company.

Railway rationalisation saw the station, the entrance to which was off Rutland Street, close in 1965, and it, together with the marshalling yards, left many acres of valuable city-centre land ripe for the redevelopments which have taken place. Train services now are concentrated on Waverley Station, in the valley below North Bridge.

The power of the steam engine – the huge expanse of land which the Caledonian Railway Company acquired at the west end of Princes Street stretched from Lothian Road to Morrison Street and Haymarket. The 'Caley' or Princes Street Station had its entrance at Rutland Street, and since its closure in 1965 the valuable railway land has been redeveloped to include the Western Approach Road and the Exchange financial centre.

Lost too is the grand Leith Central Station at the foot of Leith Walk, closed in 1952 but not demolished until 1989, its site now housing a supermarket and Leith Waterworld.

Most of the more than 50 passenger stations which were served by various suburban routes from the Caley and Waverley are now mere names, some with traces of rail platforms: Barnton, Bonnington Road, Colinton, Davidson's Mains, Gorgie East, House o' Hill Halt (Corbiehill Avenue), Meadowbank, Piershill, Powderhall, Scotland Street and Trinity, to mention just a few.

The first railway to serve the city ran from Dalkeith to the St Leonard's Yard, and that line was constructed in the 1820s and 1830s. It was called the 'Innocent Railway', reputedly because of its good safety record, and carried passengers for around 30 years and freight for a further century until the 1960s. The tunnel and trackway now provide a walkway and cycle path, starting along the edge of Holyrood Park.

The transformation of the former rail property off Lothian Road was matched by the ongoing regeneration of the Fountainbridge/Tollcross area, where half of Earl Grey Street and Riego Street were swept away in a major road-widening to open up the Tollcross junction. Goldberg's store, in the 1960s a striking example of how eye-catching a modern store could look, the old Labour Exchange, the SMT garage which stood at the end of East

Fountainbridge, the Palladium Theatre in the same street – all have been replaced by commercial and domestic properties which have transformed the character of an area recorded as far back as 1439.

The top of Lothian Road had its own regeneration in the 1930s, when the Union Canal basins of Port Hopetoun and Port Hamilton were infilled to provide land for, among other things, Lothian House. The canal basin area itself has seen a transformation with a striking project round the former Lochrin basin, Edinburgh Quay. The view down Fountainbridge will be altered again when the brewery site is cleared and new houses, hotels, shops and whatever else the planners have in mind rise on that land.

Fountainbridge was once an area of small farms, nursery gardens and orchards. One of the interesting old buildings which has vanished was Castle Barns, standing in Morrison Street at the end of Semple Street. It was probably originally a grange, or farm, connected with the Castle. The old building had forestairs, once a feature of many old Edinburgh houses, and a pantiled roof. Like so much of old Fountainbridge, it has gone.

Just up the road from Tollcross, the past few years have seen the 'loss' of the stark 1960s block which stood at the junction of Lauriston Street and Lady Lawson Street, 'a perfunctory concrete slab office', as *The Buildings of Scotland* puts it. Few tears were shed when the building used by the National Coal Board vanished to make way for two hotels.

At the foot of Lady Lawson Street stands Argyle House, which stretches up the roadway to the corner of West Port. To make way for the government offices and 'overflow' courtrooms for the Sheriff Court, old property, including Tanner's Close, where the notorious murderers William Burke and William Hare operated in the late 1820s, went – a bit of history with a nasty smell to it gone for ever.

In Lauriston Place, too, changes on a big scale are under way which will see the former Royal Infirmary site there provide the biggest city-centre renewal

after the Scottish Parliament complex. The original Baronial-style hospital, started in 1872, is protected externally at least, but many of the ancillary buildings which sprung up in the hospital grounds bounded by Lauriston Place, Chalmers Street, the Meadows and the Middle Meadow Walk have already disappeared as the Quartermile project starts to take shape. The Florence Nightingale Nurses' Home, at the foot of Archibald Place, was one of the first to be razed.

These changes are being brought about by the decision to build a new Royal Infirmary, Edinburgh's third, on the green fields of Little France, on the south side of the city.

Hospitals, more used to dealing with human casualties, have themselves been casualties over the years in the National Health Service rationalisation process, and the list of the lost includes the Northern General in Ferry Road; the Bruntsfield in Whitehouse Loan; the Eastern General at Seafield; Leith Hospital; the City Hospital at Colinton Mains; Princess Margaret Rose at Fairmilehead; the Longmore at Salisbury; Elsie Inglis Memorial at Abbeyhill; and the Deaconess in the Pleasance. In some cases, they have gone altogether and have been replaced by housing; in others, the substantial stone buildings have been converted into flats or used as offices.

The axe may also be hanging over the Royal Victoria Hospital site at Comely Bank, with the hospital moved into the Western General Hospital complex nearby.

OPPOSITE TOP.
Port Hopetoun was one of the principal basins for the Union Canal, which provided a useful waterway from Edinburgh to Falkirk, where it linked with the Forth and Clyde Canal to Glasgow. Port Hopetoun was infilled in the 1930s and Lothian House built there at the top of Lothian Road. The other terminus basin of Port Hamilton at Fountainbridge was on ground now covered by housing and commercial developments behind Gardners Crescent. A millennium project and a redevelopment of the Lochrin basin area at Fountainbridge has brought new life to the canal, which opened to horse-drawn barge and passenger boat traffic in 1822.

OPPOSITE BELOW.
A link with the far-off days when Fountainbridge had flourishing orchards and nursery gardens, Castle Barns was probably originally a grange or farm serving Edinburgh Castle. It stood in Morrison Street at the end of Semple Street.

OVERLEAF.
The Royal Infirmary moved to a huge purpose-built hospital in Lauriston Place in the 1870s from its Infirmary Street base. The first public hospital with six beds was opened in 1729 in a house at the top of Robertson's Close, off the Cowgate. The first Royal Infirmary was opened in its new building in 1741. With the new Royal Infirmary now at Little France on the south side of the city, the Lauriston site, on the northern edge of the Meadows, is being redeveloped.

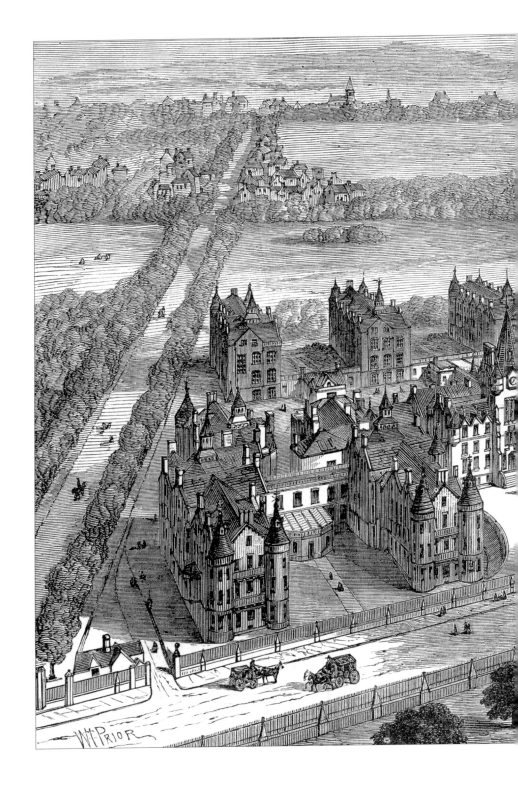

CHAPTER 22

'HURTFUL TEMPTATIONS'

It can safely be said of Edinburgh that with a few exceptions – the 'notorious hole in the ground' in Castle Terrace, where an opera house was never built is the classic – the grass does not grow under the feet of the developers.

If there is an opportunity to transform a former commercial property, whether by demolition or rehabilitation into housing, it is not long before they are chapping at the planners' door and the result of their successful overtures are all around. Indeed in the thoughts of many Edinburgh citizens the question often is: 'How did they get away with that?'

Edinburgh is a restless place, conscious of its past, confident in its future, with grandiose proposals for the 21st century which will bring about tremendous changes in the city as we see it now.

OPPOSITE TOP.
Lauriston House, the office block which stood at the junction of Lady Lawson Street and Lauriston Street, was a 1960 design by Rowand Anderson, Kininmonth & Paul. Its demolition was scarcely mourned, and the site is now occupied by two hotels.

OPPOSITE MIDDLE.
When William Burke and William Hare struck on their ploy for easy money in a serial killing spree in 1828, many of their victims were enticed back to Hare's lodging house in Tanner's Close, off the West Port, to be 'burked' (smothered). The bodies were then sold to Dr Robert Knox's assistants so the distinguished anatomist had specimens for his crowded classes of medical students. Justice caught up with the two Irishmen, and Burke was hanged in January 1829, but Hare, by turning King's Evidence against his partner in crime, escaped the gallows.

OPPOSITE BELOW.
The Princes Margaret Rose Hospital was a victim of health cutbacks. The site at Frogston Road West at Fairmilehead had a number of additions to the original buildings designed by Reginald Fairlie and constructed between 1928 and 1938. Now the site is devoted to housing, some in preserved parts of the former orthopaedic hospital.

On the north side, a transformation of poor housing, rundown industrial sites and waste ground is already under way in the Waterfront Project, which stretches from the former Granton gasworks to meet the burgeoning housing boom in the regenerated area of Leith Docks.

Two of the shoreline's most distinctive landmarks, the gas holders, have gone. Leith Fort's twin 21-storey-high housing blocks are a distant memory at the other end of the road. Already, the rebirth of the Granton Harbour precincts can be seen with much more to come.

In the spring of 2005, another familiar sight went when Capelaw Court, one of three 15-storey-tall Council housing blocks at Oxgangs, was demolished in a spectacular controlled explosion. The neighbouring Caerketton and Allermuir Courts, named, like Capelaw, after peaks in the Pentland Hills to the south of the city, have also been razed.

They were blocks of the 1960s and their days were over. The Council itself has restarted building houses, and was prepared to let housing associations have the land of its demolished homes to take on the new-build. Thus, Niddrie and Craigmillar estates and parts of West Granton and other pretty bleak areas can be revitalised for the better.

An urban village has been created between McDonald Road and Annandale Street, using mostly 'brown field' sites with the redevelopment of light industry and commercial properties. Among the buildings in that area is the Lothian Buses depot Central Garage. Its red-brick façade and huge glass dome are a reminder that it was originally put up for the Edinburgh Exhibition Association in 1922 and later converted to its garage use.

Nearby, the substantial area once occupied as the then LRT's transport depot (1974), with its strictly utilitarian buildings, has been the centre of a planning battle between local householders, community groups and would-be developers to ensure an acceptable redevelopment proposal.

The other major city-centre regeneration has started at Fountainbridge, with the new housing and office building round the derelict Lochrin Basin of the Union Canal. The removal of the massive Fountain Brewery will see the entire area, from the old Palais-de-Danse to Dundee Street, changed out of all recognition in the next few years. Again, there will be a good proportion of housing as things change along Fountainbridge.

OPPOSITE.

Going, going ... a controlled explosion brought about the demolition of Capelaw Court at Oxgangs, in 2005. A large crowd, many former residents of the tower block, watched the collapse and there were tears in many eyes as their old homes literally bit the dust.

Another once-renowned plant connected with the drink trade, the North British Distillery off Slateford Road, has gone with houses rising there. Just as they did on the former Caledonian Distillery site in Dalry Road.

The Princes Street valley is also ripe for changes at its eastern end. Already, a new office, has brought together many of the City Council's departments spread in various offices into one centre, on part of what was the car park of Waverley Station. Directly across New Street, the red-brick garage has vanished and will be replaced by a new layout of streets, houses and shops leading through the Canongate.

The sports ground at Meggetland has been renovated, with new facilities for games, but also (despite strong local opposition) with housing on a portion of the land beside the Union Canal.

And so it goes on. Something will have to happen to the now empty New St Andrew's House, by the St James' Centre. Many would like to see it pulled down, its dominance over the views from so many parts jarring on the eye. Other unsightly blocks of the same era, the 1960s and 1970s, are also likely to be demolished.

The changing scene reflects the prosperity of the city, where a modern penthouse flat can be as fiercely sought after as a detached villa in Merchiston or the Grange; where now substandard Council housing is being replaced (there are plans to sweep away literally thousands of its run-down houses in Pennywell, Gracemount, Sighthill, Royston, Wardieburn and Leith Fort); where new office blocks soar, although some stand empty for a long time.

In 1849 Lord Cockburn, the distinguished and vociferous citizen whom we have come across several times, wrote 'A Letter to the Lord Provost on the Best Ways of Spoiling the Beauty of Edinburgh.'

He railed against many of the developments he felt had been wrong for the city – the arrival of the railway in Princes Street Gardens, the destruction of trees, and particularly the loss of 'historical remains' such as the Trinity Hospital and Trinity College Church.

'Many of them are gone, many are going,' he told Lord Provost William Ivory. 'The antiquarian soul sighs over their disappearance, and forgives nothing to modern necessities. Where they are private property, which no one will purchase to prevent, they must be dealt with according to the pleasure of the owner.

'Thus many interesting memorials perish, the extinction of which may be regretted, but can neither be blamed nor prevented. But public memorials ought never to be sacrificed without absolute necessity.'

His Lordship summed up his feelings in a very telling way:

How will Edinburgh look in 1949, or in 2049? Periods far off to us; but they will arrive; and those who live with them will wonder how any other periods were ever cared for. How will it look one hundred years hence? I hope well. But I see hurtful temptations at many points. At so many, that, if not resisted, they must make all that those then alive may read or see in pictures, of what Edinburgh once was, incredible and imcomprehensible.

Edinburgh has changed in so many ways since Lord Cockburn wrote his letter, and the Cockburn Association, named after him, is a vigorous conservation body in the city. Tighter planning controls have also come into play, and the Old Town and New Town areas are recognised as a World Heritage Site.

But what else will be lost before 2049 is unanswerable. It can only be hoped that the best of the old will be preserved, and the new will be good.

BIBLIOGRAPHY

Abercrombie, Patrick and Plumstead, Derek: *A Civic Survey and Plan for the City & Royal Burgh of Edinburgh*

Arnold, Thomas: *History of the Cross of Edinburgh*

Arnot, Hugo: *The History of Edinburgh*

Baillie, Simon J: *The Private World of Cammo*

Baines, Annie Mary: *History of Dublin Street Baptist Church, Edinburgh 1858–1958*

Book of the Old Edinburgh Club: *Various volumes*

Burns, Archibald: *Picturesque 'Bits' from Old Edinburgh*

Butler, D.: *The Tron Kirk of Edinburgh*

Chambers, Robert: *Edinburgh Papers*

Chambers, Robert: *Reekiana: Minor Antiquities of Edinburgh*

Chambers, Robert: *Traditions of Edinburgh*

Chambers, Robert: *Walks in Edinburgh*

Cockburn, Henry (Lord): *Memorials of his Time*

Cockburn Henry (Lord): *A Letter to the Lord Provost on the Best Ways of Spoiling the Beauty of Edinburgh*

Creech, William: *Edinburgh Fugitive Pieces*

Dunlop, Alison Hay: *Anent Old Edinburgh*

Edinburgh Town Council: *Edinburgh 1329–1929*

Edinburgh and Leith Post-Office Directories

Footman, Ray and Young Bruce: *Edinburgh University. An Illustrated Memoir*

Geekie, Walter: *Geekie's Etchings*

Gifford, John, McWilliam, Colin and Walker, David: *The Buildings of Scotland. Edinburgh*

Glendinning, Miles and MacKechnie, Aonghus: *Scottish Architecture*

Grant, James: *Old and New Edinburgh*

Gray, John G., ed.: *The South Side Story*

Gray, W. Forbes: *Historic Churches of Edinburgh*

Harris, Stuart: *The Place Names of Edinburgh*

Holmes, Heather and Finkelstein, David, ed: *Thomas Nelson and Sons. Memories of an Edinburgh Publishing House*

Home, Bruce J.: *Old Buildings in Edinburgh*

Keir, David, ed.: *The City of Edinburgh. The Third Statistical Account of Edinburgh*

Keir, David: *The Younger Generations*

Lees, J. Cameron: *St Giles', Edinburgh. Church, College and Cathedral*

Mair, William: *Historic Morningside*

Maxwell, Sir Herbert: *Edinburgh. A Historical Study*

Miller, Robert: *Municipal Buildings of Edinburgh 1145–1895*

Robertson, David: *The Princes Street Proprietors*

Robertson, David and Wood, Marguerite: *Castle and Town*

Royal Commission on the Ancient and Historical Monuments of Scotland: *The City of Edinburgh*

Skinner, Robert T.: *The Royal Mile. Castle to Holyrood*

Smith, Mrs J. Stewart: *The Grange of St Giles*

Storer, J. and H.S.: *Views in Edinburgh and Its Vicinity*

The Life Association of Edinburgh: *Princes Street, Edinburgh*

Thomas, Brendon: *The Last Picture Shows, Edinburgh*

Wilson, Sir Daniel: *Memorials of Edinburgh in the Olden Time*

Youngson, A.J.: *The Making of Classical Edinburgh*

And the infinite resources of the Edinburgh Room in the Central Library, George IV Bridge – a treasure trove of information with a dedicated and most helpful staff.

INDEX